Gather
'ROUND THE
TABLE

WITHDRAWN FROM
RAPIDES PARISH LIBRARY

*ALA Editions purchases fund advocacy,
awareness, and accreditation programs
for library professionals worldwide.*

Gather 'Round the Table

Food Literacy Programs, Resources, and Ideas for Libraries

HILLARY DODGE

CHICAGO | 2020

HILLARY DODGE is a lifelong lover of books and food. When not eating or reading, she can most likely be found wandering into places she shouldn't and meeting characters that would raise an eyebrow. One of the greatest joys in life is exploration, she'd tell you. So go out and explore and try some of the cheese while you're there. Hillary is currently the director of the north region of the Pikes Peak Library District in Colorado Springs, Colorado.

© 2020 by the American Library Association

Extensive effort has gone into ensuring the reliability of the information in this book; however, the publisher makes no warranty, express or implied, with respect to the material contained herein.

ISBN: 978-0-8389-4629-9 (paper)

Library of Congress Control Number: 2019040962

Cover design by Alejandra Diaz. Imagery ©Adobe Stock.
Text design and composition by Karen Sheets de Gracia in the Mercury, Vista, and Wicked Grit typefaces.

⊚ This paper meets the requirements of ANSI/NISO Z39.48-1992 (Permanence of Paper).

Printed in the United States of America
24 23 22 21 20   5 4 3 2 1

 **This book is dedicated to** my husband, Mark, without whom I might never have tried beets, and my daughter, Olivia, my beautiful little goofball who never ceases to make me smile. Thanks for joining me on this great adventure.

CONTENTS

Preface How This Book Came About *ix*

Introduction Come and Get It! *xi*

Part I "FROM SOUP TO NUTS"

1. What Is Food Literacy? *3*
2. Food Movements Every Librarian Should Know *11*
3. A Primer to the Field of Culinary Arts *21*

Part II "TAKE THE CAKE"

4. The Community Food Assessment *29*
5. Food Literacy Quick-Start Guide *39*

Part III "THE PROOF IS IN THE PUDDING"

6. Short Orders *47*
7. House Specials *61*

Conclusion Go Forth and Bake It *95*

Appendixes

Appendix A COLLECTION DEVELOPMENT *97*
Appendix B TOOLS FOR THE COMMUNITY FOOD ASSESSMENT *103*
Appendix C INTERACTIVE WEBSITES, TOOL KITS, AND MOOCS *109*

About the Contributors *115*

Index *119*

PREFACE

HOW THIS BOOK CAME ABOUT

In 2016, my husband, daughter, and I decided to pursue a lifelong dream. My husband and I quit our jobs, sold our house and nearly everything in it, and shipped our car to the other side of the hemisphere. On the other end, we met it in Santiago, Chile, a country our little family of three would be calling home for the next two years.

Our dream was to write a cookbook—but not just any cookbook. We wanted to dig into the historical and cultural context of my husband's native cuisine and, in the process, capture recipes that were disappearing from the food landscape of Chile. So we drove the length of Chile, making friends and meeting fellow food enthusiasts from all walks of life. We were invited into homes and kitchens where we would ask our hosts to cook us a meal their mothers used to make. And then, with cameras and notebooks, we would observe, ask questions, and then sit down to eat with our new friends.

It was a fantastic adventure and humbling experience. In the arid *altiplanos* of the north, we dined with descendants of the Aymara people in a part of Chile that used to be Peru, eating llama *tamals* and *kalapulka*, a traditional beef and pork stew reserved for festivals and celebrations, aromatic with spices and herbs we'd never seen in our lives. In the fertile lakes region just south of the central valley of Santiago, we ate *curanto en hoyo*, a feast of seafood and pork cooked in a smoking hole in the ground beneath the pungent *nalca* leaves that were as big as a kitchen table, and afterward, just down the road, we enjoyed raspberry kuchen for dessert. In the far south, in the wet and windswept land of Patagonia and Tierra del Fuego, we watched as a lamb was slaughtered and strung across an *x* of wood, tilted just so above a firepit for hours as it cooked, a meal that would feed many, *cordero al palo*.

Along the way, I became interested in how we see and use food, how food knowledge is passed on from one generation to the next, and how the disruptive factors of a modern world make family meals challenging. In the United States, it's easy to pop around the corner and buy a frozen meal from the grocery and even easier to grab a bag of takeout. But aside from questionable nutritional value and strange additives, those meals aren't fulfilling in the way home-cooked meals are. But not everyone knows how to make a home-cooked meal.

Around the time we were wrapping up our research and preparing to return to the States, I received an issue of *Public Libraries* in the mail. Flipping through its pages, I got to thinking about food programming in libraries, and I began to wonder what was out there on the topic. As I began to search, I quickly came to see that although the topic of food and cooking in libraries was popular, there was no single resource, no book of examples, how-to guides, or even basic reference information about how to design and implement a food program or service in the library.

And that is where this book comes in. Luckily, ALA Editions agreed with me, and together we embarked on the journey of creating this book. With the help of a hugely supportive editorial and marketing team, I reached out to ALA members across the nation to connect with librarians and library paraprofessionals who were using and making food in their libraries. Their stories can be found within the pages of this book as examples of food literacy programs and services that meet the needs of a diverse range of communities around the country.

INTRODUCTION

COME AND GET IT!

Simply put, if you love libraries, food, and people, this book is for you. As mentioned previously, this book is meant to be an all-in-one resource to learn about the potential for food literacy in libraries. As such, it will appeal to a broad cross section of library and culinary professionals, including those specializing in programming, reference, collection development, archives, museums, outreach, and community engagement. Beyond libraries, this book will have resources that can also serve culinary educators, literacy coaches, civic activists, and students.

I'll approach the topic in three ways: by deconstructing the concept of food literacy into its key components and demonstrating connections within the culinary arts world, by digging into the process of a community needs assessment and providing a quick-start guide to planning and implementation, and by sharing tangible examples of programs and services, both large and small in scope, in a variety of library settings that could be used as road maps for success.

Part 1, "From Soup to Nuts," is just that: the *ABC*s of food literacy. I'll explain the term and its origin, and then I'll break it down into its component pieces, or domains. This part will also present a handful of key food movements and accompanying terminology that you've probably already heard but maybe would like to understand better. And finally, because not all of us grew up in restaurants, I'll open the door to the culinary arts world and explain how things work, define the various roles and professions within the industry, and talk about culinary education.

In Part 2, "Take the Cake," I'm going to show you how to design and implement successful food literacy programs and services in your own library. I'll start with an in-depth discussion of the benefits of a community food assessment. Then I'll guide you through the process step-by-step, from building a team and defining your scope to planning and conducting research. Following that is a quick-start guide for designing and implementing a food program or service in response to a community need. This section is filled with a lot of tools that you can get started using right away.

Part 3, "Proof Is in the Pudding," is especially exciting because it's filled with real-world examples. I've divided this part into two sections: "Short Orders" features smaller-scope services and one-off programs, such as cooking demonstrations, nutrition classes, and hands-on contests; "House Specials" features larger-scope services and programs, such as cookbook book clubs, food business workshops, and library-led community gardens. No matter the size of your library or the makeup of your community, you are bound to find great ideas to tuck into.

Finally, in the last bit of the book, I offer a couple of appendixes with collection management and program planning tools as well as further resources and contributor bios for all those who shared their food literacy projects with me.

Food is a topic that appeals to library customers of all ages and life stages, but for various (and outdated) reasons, it hasn't been at the forefront of library services. In the past, issues of safety, cleanup, and old-fashioned notions of what libraries should be have prevented food programs from taking hold. And if it was allowed in the building at all, food was mostly used to lure patrons into our programs or entice them to join in community focus groups. But the power of food doesn't stop there, as this book will illustrate.

In this age of modern libraries, public librarians are easing up on the barriers that prevented them from exploring more innovative and creative services and programs, such as makerspaces—collaborative work spaces with specialized tools and technology—and food labs. It is my hope that you'll find this book to be a valuable resource in learning about food literacy and in engaging your community in its food information needs.

PART I

"FROM SOUP TO NUTS"

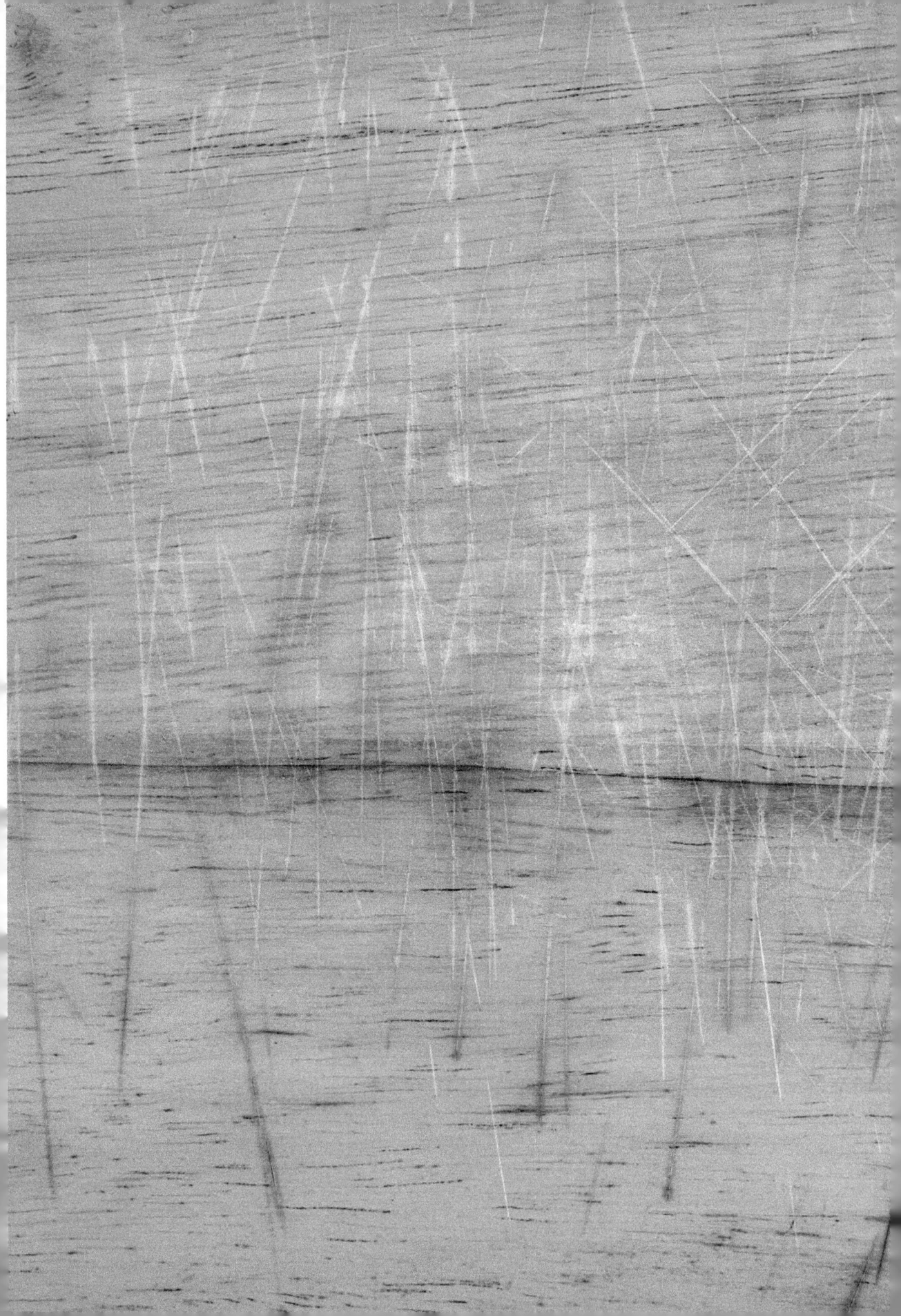

WHAT IS FOOD LITERACY?

Food is a basic human need. We eat for a number of reasons—to fill our stomachs, nourish our bodies, participate in a social or cultural event, or practice a religious belief. What we eat depends on this context and the context of a number of different interrelated conditions at the individual, household, community, national, and global levels. For example, an individual's income, a community's proximity to fresh produce, a nation's policy on food distribution and storage, and a global market environment all play into the systems that make food available and affordable or not. Further complicating this food system are different cooking styles, food trends, education accessibility, scientific discoveries and developments, and political movements at all levels.

In an effort to make such a complicated system relatable, the term "food literacy" emerged. Interestingly, the first time the term reared its head, it was thrust into the spotlight with no firm definition or defined parts, identified as a goal by the American Dietetic Association in its 1990 response to a senate inquiry on food labeling.[1] In the following years, "food literacy" and similar terms began to surface with attached definitions in a variety of professional and educational literature of multiple industries, organizations, and governments.

Today, "food literacy" is still a somewhat subjective term. Some industries apply the term to a finite set of skills, whereas others use it to encapsulate a much broader set of experiences. The most comprehensive and scalable definition to date among all the competing interpretations and uses would be Australian public health nutritionist Helen Vidgen's definition and components.[2] Dr. Vidgen's study of the term and her subsequent research into the various appearances and uses of it in health and policy literature have resulted in a solid research-supported definition. And it is this definition that this book will be referencing throughout.

A Definition and Its Parts

According to Helen Vidgen's studies, food literacy is best defined as a "collection of inter-related knowledge, skills and behaviors required to plan, manage, select, prepare, and eat foods to meet needs and determine intake. Food literacy is the scaffolding that empowers individuals, households, communities or nations to protect diet quality through change, and support dietary resilience over time."[3]

In a way, food literacy can be understood as a range of literacies required for the various processes, skills, and experiences related to food and eating in everyday life. The concept can be divided into four domains: planning and management, selection, preparation, and eating. Each domain, in turn, can be subdivided into two to three components, or subcategories, that encompass a distinct set of knowledge and skills that fall within that overall domain.

Within the domain of planning and management are the subcategories of prioritizing available resources for food, planning food intake, and making informed decisions based on needs and available resources. What this amounts to is understanding one's available time, money, and skills and using these to plan for and meet the food needs of an individual or group. This does not necessarily imply that the decisions made meet health needs; it merely means that food and meals are planned in advance. Although it goes without saying, healthy meals are easier to prepare and serve when conscious consideration is given to the planning and executing of the meals. And from a nutritional perspective, planning and management are a crucial domain to changing unhealthy patterns of eating.

The domain of selection is subdivided into the subcategories of accessing food, determining the makeup of a food product, and judging the quality of a food or food product. This domain focuses on access and understanding the food systems that are at play in the availability and affordability of food. It means understanding the advantages and disadvantages of various food sources or understanding systems to access food when money and time are in short supply. At a more granular level, it means being able to read and understand food labels, identify ingredients used in food products, know how best to store and use a food item, and make a determination on a product's healthiness.

Preparation is the domain most closely associated with the term "culinary literacy." It involves the subcategories of demonstrating kitchen skills with quality outcomes and applying kitchen safety and hygiene. Quality outcomes are key with this domain. Being able to prepare and cook a good-tasting meal is what counts. This ability includes an understanding of kitchen equipment and methods of preparation. It also involves artistic touches, such as garnishing and plating. A high level of

CHAPTER 1: WHAT IS FOOD LITERACY? 5

Table 1.1 **Food literacy in a nutshell**

Domain	Components	Application examples
1. Planning and management	Prioritizing resources for food	Setting aside time and money for food
	Planning food intake	Making a meal plan for the week
	Making informed decisions about food	Choosing whole foods over processed foods
2. Selection	Accessing food	Knowing the difference between foods available at a convenience store and the local farmers market
	Determining what's in a food product	Being able to read and understand a food label
	Judging the quality of food	Being able to tell when a fruit is ripe and knowing how long it can be stored
3. Preparation	Demonstrating kitchen skills	Knowing how to use a knife to make different cuts
	Applying kitchen safety and hygiene	Understanding how to avoid food contamination
4. Eating	Understanding the impact of food choices	Understanding the nutritional difference between choosing a soda versus a glass of water
	Demonstrating self-awareness of health and food needs	Knowing to prepare meals low in sugar if diabetes runs in the family
	Being able to join others and eat socially	Demonstrating social awareness when eating with others

skill in this domain also results in the ability to adapt to changes in environment and access to kitchen tools and equipment in order to produce predictable outcomes in meal preparation.

The final domain, eating, aside from being the most satisfying, is also the most individual. Subcategories included within this domain relate to personal well-being. They include understanding the impact of food choices, demonstrating self-awareness of health and food needs, and being able to join others and eat in a social way.

> ## RELATED TERMS
>
> In lay communication, many of these terms are used interchangeably. But it is important to realize that many of these terms came into use from a distinct industry-based perspective, and as such, professional use of these terms is often limited to that industry's understanding of the terminology.
>
> **Culinary literacy** is concerned with the skills involved in preparing and cooking foods.
>
> **Foodwork** is used to describe a set of domestic skills involved in the process of meal selection, including shopping, preparation, cooking, and eating. This term is often used from a sociology context.
>
> **Health literacy** is characterized by the development of skills and capacities that enable individuals and communities to obtain, process, and understand basic health information, including services, required to make health-related decisions. Health literacy is normally viewed through two lenses: that of the individual and that of the community.
>
> **Nutrition literacy** focuses on food intake, how the body converts food into nutrients and waste, and how the body uses nutrients for growth, development, and health.

This domain ties eating and the consequences of eating together. It connects nutrition and health literacies with self-efficacy and balance. The social aspect of eating is also crucial to this domain; eating communally lends to a sense of well-being and inclusion. In both family and larger group settings, cooking and eating together has been connected to improved health and wellness outcomes as a direct result of the need to plan for these larger meals.

Why Does a Definition Matter?

Defining food literacy helps us break down the term into its component parts or domains to allow us to see the various facets that are at play. From farm to stomach, food moves across the purviews of multiple disciplines. Having a common understanding of a term allows for easier exploration and application of the term and its components within various fields of study and production.

Food literacy is a topic of interest in national and international policy. The term has been used in Canada's *What's to Eat?* report, the European Union's discussion paper on sustainable food consumption, and the United States Institute of Medicine's committee report *Accelerating Progress in Obesity Prevention*, among others.[4]

Alongside policy, the term "food literacy" is used in application-based contexts by governments and practitioners. For instance, in the human services sector, food literacy is aligned with workforce development and life skills. In the agriculture and production sectors, it is a term that helps define food systems, environmental impact, and sustainability. Governments capitalize on the term in relation to food tourism and culture.

In regard to responding to literacy gaps, having a defined term also opens possibilities for pinpointing exact needs and being able to understand the approaches that can be taken to meet the needs. Definitions allow us as library professionals to speak to our stakeholders, our community, and each other from a common point of understanding.

Food Literacy in Libraries

Libraries not only are home to information champions but also have a long history of being propagators of social good. "Social good" is defined as an action that provides a benefit to the general public. As such, libraries have served as hosts, promoters, and also designers of social good. Think about the programs and services that libraries have created or enabled to support or directly benefit their communities: storytimes with literacy tips, book clubs, teen councils and volunteer programs, adult education classes, and many more.

Food literacy is yet another kind of social good that libraries have begun to offer their communities. Food literacy ties into a library's mission by supporting and educating for multiple literacies, including reading (reading recipes), mathematics (measurement conversions), kitchen science (safety and sanitation), and health literacy (understanding a nutrition label). Food literacy initiatives in libraries also support and improve community health as well as serve and engage as another form of community making. Some of the more common examples have included book clubs focused on cookbooks, health and nutrition workshops, and hot-plate cooking demos. More recently, libraries have upped their game through summer lunch programs, mobile kitchens, and community gardens.

One of the most progressive and perhaps best-known examples of a library taking on food literacy is the aptly named Culinary Literacy Center in the Philadelphia Free Public Library. The first of its kind in the US, the center "was created with the understanding that cooking and eating are educational acts."[5] It was designed in response to a social need within the greater Philadelphia community—not just in terms of literacy but also in regard to building community and bringing people together to sustain it. The programs and series that the center has developed do just that. For example, in their Edible Alphabet class students can acquire English, Spanish, Italian, or Mandarin language skills by learning to cook a culturally relevant meal using recipes and instruction in that language. (For libraries looking to

> **ESSENTIAL COLLECTION**
> **The Science and Sociology of Food**
>
> Alton Brown, chef and television host, made cooking fun again by explaining the science and history behind certain foods and meals. Have the same experience with these fun titles.
>
> - *Did You Just Eat That? Two Scientists Explore Double-Dipping, the Five-Second Rule, and Other Food Myths in the Lab.* Dawnson, Paul, and Sheldon, Brian.
> - *A Moveable Feast: Ten Millennia of Food Globalization.* Kiple, Kenneth.
> - *On Food and Cooking: The Science and Lore of the Kitchen.* McGee, Harold.
> - *Moveable Feasts: The History, Science, and Lore of Food.* McNamee, Gregory.
> - *Salt, Fat, Acid, Heat: Mastering the Elements of Good Cooking.* Nosrat, Samin.
> - *Cooked: A Natural History of Transformation.* Pollan, Michael.
> - *The Omnivore's Dilemma: A Natural History of Four Meals.* Pollan, Michael.
> - *Gulp: Adventures on the Alimentary Canal.* Roach, Mary.
> - *Ratio: The Simple Codes behind the Craft of Everyday Cooking.* Ruhlman, Michael.
> - *Catching Fire: How Cooking Made Us Human.* Wrandman, Richard.

embark on a similar journey, the Free Library of Philadelphia has created a step-by-step guide, "Culinary Literacy: A Toolkit for Public Libraries," available on their website for free.)

But even libraries without $1.2 million commercial kitchens have been finding ways to offer food literacy programs to their communities. The Camden County Library System in New Jersey offers Books and Cooks, a mobile kitchen program that focuses on healthy eating and consumer literacy and serves a community with only one grocery store and a number of street-corner bodegas.[6] Flavor Lab, out of the Chattanooga Public Library in Tennessee, operates their program using a Charlie Cart, a successfully kick-started kitchen on a cart, a primary goal of which is to train teens on how to cook the foods available to them in the summers when school lunches aren't available and parents are at work.

Food literacy can be scaled even smaller. Seed libraries are popping up all across the nation—both within small communities (Missoula Public Library; Montana and Richmond Public Library, California) and cities (Pikes Peak Library

District, Colorado)—with the goal of enabling personal and community gardens through classes and seed sharing.[7] Fort Hays State University in Kansas has the Tiger Food Exchange—located on the first floor of Forsyth Library—a food pantry dedicated to eradicating student food insecurity via a university garden and community donations.[8] Ottawa Public Library in Ontario, Canada, has rolled out their food literacy project, Á la Carte, in the form of an online resource center geared toward helping patrons learn from and connect with food movers and shakers within their city.[9] And at the very least, nearly every library is already providing food literacy through the thoughtful curation of their collections.

As our world continues to change and our communities with it, it is important for libraries to think ahead about their value and purpose. With consumer markets becoming even trickier to navigate and understand, will we help our users meet their food literacy needs? Will we empower them to make the best choices for themselves, their community, and the environment? Can we respond to the changing shape of the global food supply and the way it impacts our most basic need for food and nutrition? By considering food literacy as an important addition to the values and services that libraries support, we can do just that.

NOTES

1. Helen Vidgen, "An Overview of the Use of the Term Food Literacy," in *Food Literacy: Key Concepts for Health and Education* (London: Routledge, 2016).
2. Helen Vidgen, ed., *Food Literacy: Key Concepts for Health and Education* (London: Routledge, 2016).
3. Helen Vidgen, "A Definition of Food Literacy and Its Components," in *Food Literacy: Key Concepts for Health and Education* (London: Routledge, 2016).
4. Alison Howard and Jessica Brichta, *What's to Eat? Improving Food Literacy in Canada* (Ottawa: Conference Board of Canada, 2013); L. A. Reisch, S. Lorek, and S. Beitz, *CORPUS Discussion Paper 2 on Policy Instruments for Sustainable Food Consumption* (Brussels, Belgium: European Commission, 2011); D. Glickman et al., *Accelerating Progress in Obesity Prevention: Solving the Weight of the Nation* (Washington, DC: National Academies Press, 2015).
5. J. Bowers, L. Fitzgerald, and S. Urminska, "Culinary Literacy: A Toolkit for Public Libraries" (Philadelphia: Free Library of Cooked to Perfection, 2015).
6. L. Ewen, "A Moveable Feast: Libraries Use Mobile Kitchens to Teach Food Literacy," *American Libraries Magazine*, September/October 2018, 12–15.
7. A. Alger, "Seed Libraries in Sustainable Communities," *Pacific Northwest Library Association Quarterly* (Fall 2014): 25–31.
8. E. Udell, "Food for Thought: Academic Libraries Are Fighting Campus Food Insecurity with Onsite Pantries," *American Libraries Magazine*, May 2019, 12–15.
9. "Á la Cart: A Food Literacy Project," Ottawa Public Library, 2017, www.biblioottawa library.ca/en/food-literacy.

FOOD MOVEMENTS EVERY LIBRARIAN SHOULD KNOW

Food deserts. Genetically modified organisms (GMOs). Farm to table. We've heard the terms before—in the news, in social media, on podcasts, even in everyday conversation. But what do they actually mean? Food has become very political, and as such, the meanings behind some of these terms have become clouded, misinterpreted, and misused. Often the terms and the language used to describe them are heavily intertwined; the web of food issues is complex and multithreaded. Having a firm understanding of the terms will enlighten the reader and get them thinking: Why should we care? Why should we care now? What place do libraries have to make a difference?

Food Allergies and Intolerances

Physiological responses to certain foods are common enough, but what's the difference between an allergic reaction and an intolerance? While intolerances are connected to the digestive process and are generally not as severe as an allergic reaction, they can certainly result in real discomfort. Food intolerances, such as a lactose intolerance, can be caused by a number of things, including the absence of an enzyme required for digestion of certain foods, sensitivity to food additives, stress, or another condition (i.e., irritable bowel syndrome or celiac disease).

Although many symptoms overlap, the key difference is that a food intolerance won't cause anaphylaxis, which can result from food allergies.[1] Common intolerances to food include dairy; gluten; caffeine; salicylates; amines; fermentable oligo-, di-, mono-saccharides and polyols (FODMAPs); sulfites; fructose; aspartame; eggs; monosodium glutamate (MSG); food colorings; yeast; and sugar alcohols.[2] Because there are so many similarities, however, it's always advised to see a physician after a food reaction to determine whether an intolerance or an allergy is at the root of the problem.

According to the National Institute of Allergy and Infectious Disease (NIAID), food allergies affect approximately 5 percent of children and 4 percent of adults in the United States.[3] A food allergy is an abnormal reaction by the immune system to a component found within food, sometimes resulting in a life-threatening response. Since 2006, the Food Allergen Labeling and Consumer Protection Act (FALCPA) requires most packaged food in the US to disclose when they contain a "major food allergen"[4] Major food allergens account for more than 90 percent of all documented food allergies in the US and include milk, eggs, fish, shellfish, tree nuts, peanuts, wheat, and soybeans.[5]

With the growing need for information, libraries have been responding to needs in education and resources about food allergies by boosting their collections in a number of ways: inclusive cookbooks, focused cookbooks, and children's fiction with characters that have food allergies or intolerances. Libraries are even offering cooking demonstrations and classes on ways to cook with substitutes. Some libraries have even embraced an allergen-free environment. At the Benton Harbor Public Library in Michigan, a food tasting program was offered to allow patrons with intolerances to taste test substitutes, a sort of try-before-you-buy educational program. For those with lactose intolerances, substitutes can be expensive, so an opportunity to try various options at no cost to the individual was a huge hit.[6]

Food Ethics and the Food System

Food ethics is an interdisciplinary field of study that is focused on guiding change and policy toward fair food systems. Ethical thinking means considering values when making choices about food—choices about our principles, our reasons for regarding a practice as right or wrong.[7] There are three areas of consideration within food ethics: well-being, autonomy, and fairness. Some of the questions that guide the field of food ethics are as follows: What will be good or bad for humans, animals, and our planet? Does the health and welfare of the human, animal, or planet have greater value than this change or system? How free should people be to make their own choices about access to foods that affect the welfare of animals, humans, or the planet? Do we produce food that is fair to everyone?[8]

These are certainly heavy questions, questions that many people have very strong feelings about. Food ethics is very much focused on food systems and consumer impact. For example, food packaging and its impact on the environment, government agricultural subsidies and the poor quality of US school lunch programs, sugar and the obesity crisis, modern agricultural practices and global warming, the meat industry—these are all examples of issues heavily discussed within food ethics.

> ## RELATED TERMS
>
> **Fair trade** is a principle within the field of food ethics as well as other fields and industries. Fair trade means that the supply chain meets specific criteria such as fair pay for workers and the opportunity to participate in the global market.
>
> **Food fraud**, which can affect a consumer's experience and health, comes in many forms: substitution of ingredients, dilution, origin masking (meat industry anyone?), brand counterfeiting, and intentional distribution of contaminated foods.[9]
>
> **Food miles**, a topic impacting global food ethics, refers to the miles a food or food product travels during its processing and distribution. For example, where do the tomatoes in our grocery come from when they are out-of-season in our community? Food miles impact an industry's carbon footprint.
>
> A **foodshed** is a geographical location that produces food for a particular population. It is used in defining an area's food system, including resources at play, food produced, processing and packaging locations, and distribution flow.*
>
> * Foodshed Alliance, "What Is a Foodshed?," 2019, http://foodshedalliance.org/what-is-a-foodshed/.

Global food ethics may seem like a daunting topic to take on at the library level, but libraries are doing just this. By hosting community discussions and lecture series, libraries are engaging their patrons in talking about the bigger picture. At the Greenwich Library in Connecticut, their FocusOn: Food series has been wildly popular. In addition to hosting authors and chefs (like award-winning journalist Mark Bittman) for lectures and presentations, they have a lecture and film series where they screen a film relating to food, followed by a lecture and discussion. For example, in April 2019, they screened Patagonia's documentary *Unbroken Ground*; the discussion that followed focused on regenerative farming and the future of food.[10]

Food Security and Combatting Food Deserts

Food security is an issue that affects individuals, households, communities, towns and cities, states and regions, countries, and continents. It is defined as a measure of food available within a group or community and an individual's access to that food supply. Factors that play into food security include income, consumption, agricultural production and distribution, market conditions, and disruptive events such as droughts, fuel shortages, economic instability, and wars.

> ## RELATED TERMS
>
> **Food justice** refers to a grassroots initiative grown from communities in response to food insecurities, focusing on racial, cultural, and socioeconomic inequalities in the food system. It looks at the food system holistically, from farm laborers to processors, shopkeepers to consumers.
>
> **Food sovereignty** is a movement that takes the approach that those who produce, distribute, and consume a food should have control and determination over the policies governing production and distribution. This perspective denies that corporations and market institutions should control the global food system. This term is often used in opposition to food security, which can rely on the efficiency and productivity of a corporate food regime to distribute food into food-insecure areas.
>
> **The green revolution** is a product of developments in plant breeding and agricultural technology between the 1960s and 1980s that resulted in improved cereal crop yields. Critics point out that while the green revolution did produce more food, it did nothing to improve access for areas in need. Additionally, increased yield was the result of technological and scientific advances, such as genetically modified plants and chemical fertilizers, which places it in direct opposition to the organic food movement.

In 1948, the United Nations recognized the "right to food" as a primary article in the Declaration of Human Rights. The term "food security" was first born during the 1974 World Food Conference in Rome, when conversations around hunger and malnutrition were a central focus and food supply was examined as a key solution. Today, food security is also very much tied to individual and community health, and as such, food security becomes a measure of healthy food available and accessible regularly. "Regularity," implying resilience to future disruption in availability, is another key component of the modern understanding of the term. According to the Food and Agriculture Organization of the United Nations (FAO), there are four components to the actualization of food security: availability, access, stability, and utilization.[11] The term "food desert" falls within the category of "access" as an indicator of food insecurity.

It makes sense that healthier diets are easier to maintain with easier access to healthy foods. But there are places in our urban and rural environments where healthy foods are hard to come by. These are called "food deserts." The USDA defines food deserts as areas with little to no access to fresh fruit, vegetables, and other healthful whole foods. These areas, usually impoverished, lack supermarkets,

CHAPTER 2: FOOD MOVEMENTS EVERY LIBRARIAN SHOULD KNOW 15

grocery stores, farmers' markets, and other health food providers.[12] Instead, residents of these areas may only have convenience stores and fast-food restaurants as the closest food options.

Food deserts are being combatted at all levels—by global food organizations, federal and local government, businesses, and community groups and activists. Responses to food deserts have been varied and include such concepts as community gardens and food rescue efforts (see later on for more on this topic). Baltimarket was a grant-funded program offered in partnership with the Baltimore City Health Department's Virtual Supermarket Program and a number of community partners, including the public library. Its purpose was to bring healthy food choices to neighborhoods identified as food deserts.[13] Community members could place orders for their groceries at their local community center or library, via a number of payment options, including SNAP EBT, and later pick up their groceries from the same location.[14]

In another example, the Northern Onondaga Public Library (NOPL), in Upstate New York, has partnered with Field Goods, a company specializing in fresh food distribution, enabling patrons to order and pick up fresh fruits, vegetables, breads, meats, and artisanal products from their local library.[15] NOPL also has a community garden at their Cicero location, which is open to everyone to learn, plant, and harvest.[16]

GMOs and the Future of Food

A GMO is a genetically modified food. That means that those foods have had specific genes altered or manipulated via genetic engineering techniques to produce a plant with desirable qualities. Desirable qualities may enable a plant to withstand drought or disease, control the weed environment around a planting, avoid or repel pests, as well as alter the nutritional quality of a food.

GMOs have been a contentious issue in the food world. Those who are anti-GMO argue that with little to no data on the long-term effects of GMOs in the food system, the use of such crops equates to a "colossal public health experiment."[17] Also, GMOs are associated with an increased use of chemicals toxic to the environment and humans and are controlled by a handful of massive multinational corporations who closely control their products.[18] GMOs are also typically produced in a monoculture environment. That means two things: first, each plant is genetically identical to another in the same planting, and second, farmers may be growing a single crop. Why this matters in the anti-GMO debate is because genetically identical plants could potentially all be wiped out by the same disease. Also, farming a single crop within an area of land is a form of intensive farming that depletes soil minerals, whereas slow farming rotates crops to better preserve the mineral content of the soil.

GMO proponents argue that pest-resistant, drought-resistant plants will mean more food for the population. They also argue that with continued genetic development, food can be made to be more nutritious. For instance, plants could be engineered to have more protein and vitamins, which would open up new dietary options for vegans and vegetarians.

Regardless of where the GMO food debate ends up, there have been other minds out there working to design and develop the new foods of the future. Many

ESSENTIAL COLLECTIONS
Hot Topics in Food

To learn more about the many terms and movements touched upon in this chapter (and many more), here are some further reading recommendations.

- *Rebuilding the Foodshed: How to Create Local, Sustainable, and Secure Food Systems.* Ackerman-Leist, Philip.
- *Never Out of Season: How Having the Food We Want When We Want It Threatens Our Food Supply and Our Future.* Dunn, Rob.
- *Sorting the Beef from the Bull: The Science of Food Fraud Forensics.* Evershed, Richard, and Temple, Nicola.
- *Fair Food: Growing a Healthy, Sustainable Food System for All.* Hesterman, Oran.
- *Plants vs. Meats: The Health, History, and Ethics of What We Eat.* Hughes, Meredith.
- *Eat Drink Vote: An Illustrated Guide to Food Politics.* Nestle, Marion.
- *Unsavory Truth: How Food Companies Skew the Science of What We Eat.* Nestle, Marion.
- *Real Food/Fake Food: Why You Don't Know What You're Eating and What You Can Do about It.* Olmsted, Larry.
- *In Defense of Food: An Eater's Manifesto.* Pollan, Michael.
- *The Stop: How the Fight for Good Food Transformed a Community and Inspired a Movement.* Saul, Nick, and Curtis, Andrea.
- *Seeds of Resistance: The Fight to Save Our Food Supply.* Shapiro, Mark.
- *Clean Meat: How Growing Meat without Animals Will Revolutionize Dinner and the World.* Shapiro, Paul.
- *Waste: Uncovering the Global Food Scandal.* Stuart, Tristam.
- *The Evolved Eater: A Quest to Eat Better, Live Better, and Change the World.* Taranto, Nick.

of these foods or food products aim to reduce waste, cut back on greenhouse emissions, and eliminate food miles and the need for mass transport. Alternatives to meat have been a big area of research and development. The meat industry's impact on the environment is nonsustainable. The ethics around meat production and processing are questionable. The traceability of meat is extremely poor; for instance, the meat of more than one thousand distinct individuals may be found within a single hamburger patty.[19] Yuck. Innovative foodies are thus devising alternatives to meat. Beyond Meat, a company that seeks to replicate the meat experience using plants, gives us "chicken" and "beef" without the animals being involved. Others have moved in the direction of insects as an alternative protein. One company, Sushi Singularity, opening in Japan in late 2019, uses lab-grown proteins to 3-D print sushi for consumption.[20]

But beyond protein, the future of food means better use of our planet's limited resources. This includes water as well as land. Agriculture will have to change to meet the growing demand for food across the world. Indoor warehouse farms, farm-to-door delivery, diets developed based on a person's genome, and appliances that receive data from wearable tech that will determine what food is best for you to consume after a workout or a Netflix binge—all have been predicted as the future of food. One thing we know for sure: in many ways, the food system is broken. But the more libraries engage with food literacy, the better off our communities will be, and the more informed and capable our patrons will be in helping make positive changes for the future.

Popular Diets [21]

Clean eating refers to a whole-food approach. Whole foods are foods that are not processed. Superfoods, or nutrient-rich foods—such as chia seeds, goji berries, and kale—are popular with this diet. Refined sugars and carbohydrates are a no-no.

Farm to table is a social movement within the world of food. It responds to two main questions: (1) How fresh and good tasting is our food? (2) How is our food produced and where does it come from? Farm-to-table eating means eating locally and seasonally, with very little intermediary processing. Generally, farm-to-table eateries and restaurants are seen as more expensive than other food options.

Low-calorie, low-fat, and low-carb diets attempt to lower the consumption of foods that contain these elements. **Low-calorie** diets are concerned with reducing the intake of calories—1 calorie is the amount of energy needed to raise the temperature of 1 kilogram of water 1 degree Celsius—as a means of weight loss. This regimen requires that dieters track the calories of the food and beverages they consume while keeping at or below a specific per-day goal. **Low-fat** diets are similar, as fat is high in calories, but are usually aimed at improving health conditions to lower disease risk. The focus is less on calorie counting and more on avoiding or limiting items containing oils, spreads, and high-fat foods. **Low-carb** diets also aim for weight loss, the theory being that carbohydrates are more easily stored as fat within the body. Dieters avoid high-carb foods such as breads, pastas, grains, and starchy vegetables.

The **Mediterranean** diet tries to emulate the foodways of the Mediterranean peoples, who are said to live longer, healthier lives than Western peoples. Traditionally, these diets limit sugar, red meat, and processed foods and focus on fresh vegetables, whole grains, olive oil, garlic, fish, fruit, and wine.

The **Paleolithic** diet takes its inspiration from the foodways of our ancient ancestors, a style of food preparation and eating that is purported to be more natural. The concept at heart here is the claim that the human digestive system would be better off if we avoided foods created by modern processing techniques, including some farming practices, which means most grains and dairy are avoided. Paleo dieters instead fill their plates with meat, leafy greens, and nuts.

Religion-based diets govern food and dining practices under a proscribed set of circumstances, which may include how a food is prepared, which days of the week have special dietary significance, or what types of food or drink may or may not be consumed. Examples include halal (Muslim) and kosher (Jewish) diets. Other religions such as Buddhism or Hinduism practice vegan or vegetarian diets.

A **vegetarian** diet avoids most animal proteins. Milk and eggs are often the exceptions. A **vegan** diet excludes all animal proteins (and edible animal products such as honey) and is often practiced beyond the consumption of food. For example, vegans may avoid purchasing items made of animal products such as leather, fur, or bone.

Libraries have embraced the desire for information on popular diets by building them into their collections. Some libraries have gone a step further. Popular diet educational series and cooking classes have begun to be offered at libraries with the aid of local universities and businesses. Many libraries that host community gardens also have classes or demonstrations about ways to cook and store the food grown in those gardens. At the Sacramento Public Library in California, children get to touch and taste the food grown in their Read-and-Feed Teaching and Demonstration Garden.[22]

Waste and Food Rescue

Food waste facts are harrowing. Here's a few to hammer home this sad reality:

- ⇨ **Roughly one-third of the food** produced in the world for human consumption is lost to waste every year—that's roughly 1.3 billion tons, or enough to feed three billion people.[23]
- ⇨ **Consumers in rich countries** (such as the US) waste almost as much food

CHAPTER 2: FOOD MOVEMENTS EVERY LIBRARIAN SHOULD KNOW 19

per year as the entire net food production of sub-Saharan Africa.[24]
- **Waste per capita** in Europe and North America is between 95 and 115 kilograms a year, or roughly 210 to 253 pounds.[25]
- **In retail environments**, large quantities of food are wasted due to appearance alone. Waste amounts to squandering much-needed resources and needlessly producing greenhouse gas emissions as food is transported but never purchased or eaten.[26]

Food rescue is all about minimizing waste in the food system and moving the saved food to points of need. Many cities have food rescue organizations that work with area producers and stores to redistribute excess food via points of access that make sense for the community. In particular, food rescue organizations often work with underserved populations and those within identified food deserts (see earlier for more on this topic).

Food pantries and church kitchens are often recipients of food rescue efforts. But new innovative platforms are expanding the reach of food rescue. Transfernation, a New York City nonprofit, launched an app in 2018 that connected those in need with food systems and distributors across the city. Essentially, the app is an on-demand food rescue service, weekly diverting 1.5 to 2.7 metric tons of food that would otherwise end up as waste in landfills to local food banks, feeding programs, shelters, and soup kitchens.[27] In library land, libraries have served as collection points for donations of canned goods, homes to mini food banks, and community-supported agriculture (CSA) distribution sites.

NOTES

1. J. Li, "What's the Difference between a Food Intolerance and a Food Allergy?," Mayo Clinic, May 23, 2019, www.mayoclinic.org/diseases-conditions/food-allergy/expert-answers/food-allergy/faq-20058538.
2. J. Kubala, "The 8 Most Common Food Intolerances," Healthline, January 25, 2018, www.healthline.com/nutrition/common-food-intolerances.
3. "Food Allergy," NIAID, 2018, https://niaid.nih.gov/diseases-conditions/food-allergy.
4. FALCPA Public Law 108–282, Title II.
5. "Food Allergen Labeling and Consumer Protection Act of 2004 Questions and Answers," FDA, 2006, www.fda.gov/guidanceregulation/guidancedocuments regulatoryinformation/allergens/ucm106890.htm.
6. K. Boyer, "Food Programs Appeal to Library Patrons," *Public Libraries Online*, May 6, 2013, http://publiclibrariesonline.org/2013/05/food-programs-appeal-to-library-patrons/.
7. "What Is Food Ethics?," Food Ethics Council, May 29, 2018, video, 1:08, https://vimeo.com/272330915.

8. "Food Ethics in Practice," Food Ethics Council, 2019, www.foodethicscouncil.org/programme/food-ethics-in-practice/.
9. Sarah Brewer, Joel Levy, and Ginny Smith, *How Food Works* (New York: DK, 2019).
10. "FocusOn: Food," Greenwich Library, 2019, www.greenwichlibrary.org/focuson-food/.
11. "Food Security Indicators," FAO, September 11, 2018, www.fao.org/economic/ess/ess-fs/ess-fadata/en/#.XRqF-fZFxPY.
12. American Nutrition Association, "USDA Defines Food Deserts," NutritionDigest, 2010, http://americannutritionassociation.org/newsletter/usda-defines-food-deserts.
13. "Baltimarket Virtual Supermarket Program," BmoreHealthy, posted July 27, 2017, YouTube video, 4:26, www.youtube.com/watch?v=QjxmzNiQfnw.
14. B. Schiller, "Baltimore's Virtual Supermarkets Bring Fruits and Vegetables to Food Deserts," Fast Company, March 16, 2017, www.fastcompany.com/3057686/baltimores-virtual-supermarkets-bring-fruits-and-veggies-to-food-deserts.
15. "Field Goods Drop-Off Locations," NOPL, 2019, www.nopl.org/about-us/community-connections/.
16. "LibraryFarm at Cicero," NOPL, 2019, www.nopl.org/services/spaces/library-farm/.
17. Brewer, Levy, and Smith, *How Food Works*.
18. "The GMO Debate," Alliance for Science, 2018, https://allianceforscience.cornell.edu/blog/2018/08/the-gmo-debate/.
19. "How Many Cattle in a Ground-Beef Patty?," FarmProgress, December 1, 2017, www.farmprogress.com/beef-quality/how-many-cattle-ground-beef-patty.
20. "Restaurant Will Serve 3D-Printed Sushi," Design Boom, March 15, 2019, www.designboom.com/technology/open-meals-3d-printed-sushi-based-on-customers-saliva-and-urine-03-15-2019/. (As a side note, I saw this at SXSW 2019 and was blown away by the delicate and beautiful creations built by the food printers.)
21. Brewer, Levy, and Smith, *How Food Works*.
22. T. Inklebarger, "Library to Farm to Table," *American Libraries*, November 1, 2016, https://americanlibrariesmagazine.org/2016/11/01/library-farm-to-table/.
23. "Food Waste Facts," Stop Wasting Food, 2019, https://stopwastingfoodmovement.org/food-waste/food-waste-facts/.
24. "Save Food: Global Initiative on Food Loss and Waste Reduction," FAO, 2019, www.fao.org/save-food/resources/keyfindings/en/.
25. "Save Food."
26. "Food Waste Facts."
27. S. Blair, "Transfernation's New App Seeks to Reduce Food Insecurity in Urban Areas," Foodtank, May 2018, https://foodtank.com/news/2018/05/transfernation-hannah-dehradunwala-food-waste/.

A PRIMER TO THE FIELD OF CULINARY ARTS

M ost of us have been the beneficiaries of an individual with a culinary education. Whether from eating at a restaurant, buying a food product at a supermarket, or being lucky enough to have a chef friend who brings amazing dishes to potlucks—most of us have been in awe of the power of cooking from one angle or another. Cooking competitions and television shows have also swept the nation as a popular form of entertainment—and naturally, have opened many peoples' eyes to the rewards and appeal of a culinary education.

According to the Bureau of Labor Statistics, the job outlook for chefs and head cooks in the United States is expected to increase by 10 percent from 2016 to 2026.[1] To pursue a career in food, there are several pathways a person can take. Those successful in the field have business acumen, communication skills, creativity, dexterity, leadership and team-player skills, physical stamina, a sense of taste and smell, and time-management skills. Many food prep and line cook positions require basic education, such as a high school diploma or equivalent or training at a technical school. To move up in the field, experience is the number-one requirement. And generally speaking, there is a difference in education between the titles of "cook" and "chef."

While some chefs can train on the job and work their way up from the entry-level positions, many chefs have received higher education in the form of technical school training or a four-year college or university degree or have participated in an apprenticeship. Apprenticeships are offered by various professional organizations, culinary institutes, industry associations, or trade unions. In the United States, the American Culinary Federation is the organization that oversees the

> ## TOP CULINARY SCHOOLS IN THE U.S.
>
> 1. The Culinary Institute of America at Hyde Park (Hyde Park, NY)
> 2. Institute of Culinary Education (New York, NY and Los Angeles, CA)
> 3. International Culinary Center (New York, NY)
> 4. Auguste Escoffier School of Culinary Arts (Austin, TX, and Boulder, CO)
> 5. L'Academie de Cuisine (Gaithersburg, MD)
> 6. Johnson and Wales University (Providence, RI, and Denver, CO)
> 7. Metropolitan Community College Nebraska (Omaha, NE)
> 8. Kendall College of Culinary Arts (Chicago, IL)
> 9. New England Culinary Institute (Montpelier, VT)
> 10. Sullivan University National Center of Hospitality Studies (Louisville, KY)
>
> This list is from "The 30 Best Culinary Schools," Best Schools, February 1, 2019, https://thebestschools.org/rankings/best-culinary-schools/.

accreditation process for culinary programs and apprenticeships. Their website provides an exhaustive database of all approved programs, apprenticeships, and non-degree-granting programs, such as workforce development and jobs corps training.

Accredited programs can also be found by searching the Higher Learning Commission, the New England Association of Schools and Colleges, the Middle States Commission on Higher Education, the Northwest Commission on Colleges and Universities, the Southern Association of Colleges and Schools's Commission on Colleges, and the Western Association of Schools and Colleges. Typical degree majors include culinary arts, pastry and baking arts, restaurant and hotel management, hospitality management, and culinary arts management. A degree program or formal training will instruct the student on cooking methods, national sanitation standards, administration and kitchen management skills, food production and processing, knife and cutlery skills, customer service, and how the culinary industry works.

Many chefs end up working in the food-service industry, which includes restaurants of all kinds, cafés, coffee shops, bars, breweries, distilleries, wineries, food trucks, and street vendors. But job opportunities and career paths don't lie solely within the realm of restaurants. There are a number of different fields and industries where an individual interested in working with food may find a position, including research and development (for instance, designing a new food product), production (developing new techniques for producing a food product), purchasing (evaluating and selecting food products for a business or organization), specialized food services (managing a food service, business, or organization), traveler accommodation (hotels and resorts), private and personal chef services, and recreation (cannabusiness, for example).

The Brigade de Cuisine

A cook will cook. A chef will do many things, including oversee kitchen and staff, receive deliveries, manage inventory, plan menus, design dishes, inspect supplies and equipment, and monitor sanitation. The modern structure of the restaurant kitchen owes its organization and titles to French chef and restaurateur Georges Auguste Escoffier. He designed a system of hierarchy based on military order, called the *brigade de cuisine*. The concept was developed to lend order and efficiency and to clarify specializations within the kitchen.[2]

The brigade is also meant to build upon the concept of mise en place, a French term that translates to "everything in its place." Mise en place is a core philosophy of professional standards within the field of culinary arts. It represents both an ethical code and a state of mind. What it amounts to is the prework and thought process that goes into the organization of the kitchen as well as the chef's immediate work surface. It can be applied to the setup of ingredients and equipment as well as to the flow and balance of preparing various things at the same time. In other words, an efficient chef is a well-organized and well-prepared chef.

RELATED TERMS

A **bartender** manages the bar, which can include beer, cocktails, spirits, and wine.

A **chef de tourant**, **swing cook**, or **relief cook** is meant to fill in wherever they are needed when stations become busy.

A **cicerone** is an individual who holds a certification and is an expert in brewing, selecting, and serving beers.

A **short-order cook** prepares quick and simple items from the menu. This is a position commonly found in cafés, franchises and fast-food restaurants, and diners. Their goal is to clear order tickets as quickly as possible while maintaining a set standard for the quality of the food ordered.

A **sommelier**, or **chef de vin**, assists guests in their selection of wines, liquors, and beers. Specifically, a sommelier is an expert in every aspect of wine selection and pairing. They hold a specialized certificate.

Within the brigade system, there are also specialized roles. The *boucher*, or "butcher," prepares cuts of meat for the other station or specialized chefs. An *entremetier*'s domain is vegetables and starches. The *garde manger*, or "keeper of the food," is responsible for cold food preps and services such as buffets, salads, fruits, cold cuts, and hors d'oeuvres. The *grillardin*, or "grill chef," oversees grilling. The pâtissier, or "pastry chef," is in charge of desserts. The *poissonier*, or "fish cook," oversees the provisioning, preparation, and cooking of seafoods. The *potager* prepares stocks, soups, and stews. A *rotisseur*, or "roast chef," cooks meats. A *saucier*, or "sauté chef," prepares sauces and gravies. This listing is not exhaustive, and within fine dining and haute cuisine establishments, there may be other specialized chefs and cooks.

There is also a parallel brigade system for the dining room, or front of house.[3] At the top is the *maître d'*, or general manager, who oversees the entire operations of the dining room. Reporting directly to the manger is the *chef de salle*, or floor supervisor. This role generally directly supervises the dining staff. The chef de salle

Table 3.1 **The brigade de cuisine**

Title	Other titles	Role
Chef de cuisine	Executive chef, head chef	Responsible for all operations within the kitchen, including supervising staff, creating menus, purchasing ingredients, and maintaining order and sanitation
Sous chef	Second chef, under chef, deputy chef	Serves as second in command, oversees food lines and stations, and may serve as *aboyeur* (expediter) during service
Chef de partie	Senior chef, station chef	Manages a particular station within the kitchen
Demi chef		Assistants to the chefs de parties, does most of the preparation of the food at a station
Cuisiner	Station cook	Cooks food within a specific station
Commis	Line cook, junior cook	Assigned to a specific station within the kitchen, cooks all food within that station and is responsible for the care of tools within station
Apprentice	Prep cook, porter, hand, kitchen assistant	May be assigned to any or various stations in rotation, performs cleaning and basic prep

ESSENTIAL COLLECTIONS
The Business of Food

These resources would be welcome additions to library collections as we fulfill our roles as information hubs not just for individuals but also for small businesses.

- *No Half Measures: A Life in Wine, Food and Travel*. Benson, Jeffrey.
- *Food and Wine Tourism, 2nd Edition*. Croce, E.
- *Start Your Own Food Truck Business: Cart Trailer Kiosk Standard and Gourmet Trucks Mobile Catering Bustaurant*. Entrepreneur Media.
- *Start Your Own Specialty Food Business: Your Step-by-Step Startup Guide to Success*. Entrepreneur Media.
- *Cooking up a Business: Lessons from Food Lovers Who Turned Their Passion into a Career—and How You Can Too*. Hofstetter, Rachel.
- *Homemade for Sale: How to Set Up and Market a Food Business from Your Home Kitchen*. Kivirist, Lisa.
- *Food on Wheels: The Complete Guide to Starting a Food Truck, Food Cart, or Other Mobile Food Business*. Lewis, Jennifer.
- *Getting Your Specialty Food Product onto Store Shelves: The Ultimate Wholesale How-to Guide for Artisan Food Companies*. Lewis, Jennifer.
- *Running a Food Truck for Dummies*. Myrick, Richard.
- *The Complete Idiot's Guide to Starting a Food Truck Business*. Philips, Alan.
- *Recipe for Success: An Insider's Guide to Bringing Your Natural Good to Market*. Steinberg, Abigail.
- *The Food Truck Handbook: Start, Grow, and Succeed in the Mobile Food Business*. Weber, David.
- *Have Fork, Will Travel*. Wolf, Erik.
- *Good Food, Great Business: How to Take Your Artisan Food Idea from Concept to Marketplace*. Wyshak, Susie.

may also be used in reference to a head waiter. The *chef d'etage*, or captain, works directly with the guests, explaining the menu, answering questions, and taking orders. The *chef de rang* ensures the table is properly set for each course and delivers the food to the table. The *demi-chef de rang* is a table busser, tasked with removing dishes and cleaning tables.

In modern restaurants, many of these positions have been combined into a single position. For example, a *hostess* will greet customers and seat them, and a *waiter* will explain the menu, take orders, and serve the food to the customers. The full brigade system, however, is still at play in many formal dining scenarios, including at fine dining and haute cuisine restaurants as well as within private clubs. Outside of the brigade system, there are other roles within the restaurant, including the owner, manager (sometimes there is a front-of-house manager overseeing the dining room and a kitchen manager overseeing the back of house operations), banquet and catering manager, dishwasher, and janitorial staff. Specialized roles may live in-house or be outsourced to other firms and businesses: marketing and promotions, interior design, sanitation and cleaning, pest control, and equipment maintenance.

NOTES

1. United States Department of Labor, "Chefs and Head Cooks," *Occupational Outlook Handbook*, 2019, www.bls.gov/ooh/food-preparation-and-serving/chefs-and-head-cooks.htm.
2. Eric T., "What Is the Kitchen Brigade?," *Culinary Lore*, March 4, 2014, https://culinarylore.com/food-history:what-is-the-kitchen-brigade/.
3. Eric T, "What Is the Dining Room Brigade System?," *Culinary Lore*, June 4, 2016, https://culinarylore.com/food-history:what-is-the-dining-room-brigade-system/.

PART II
"TAKE THE CAKE"

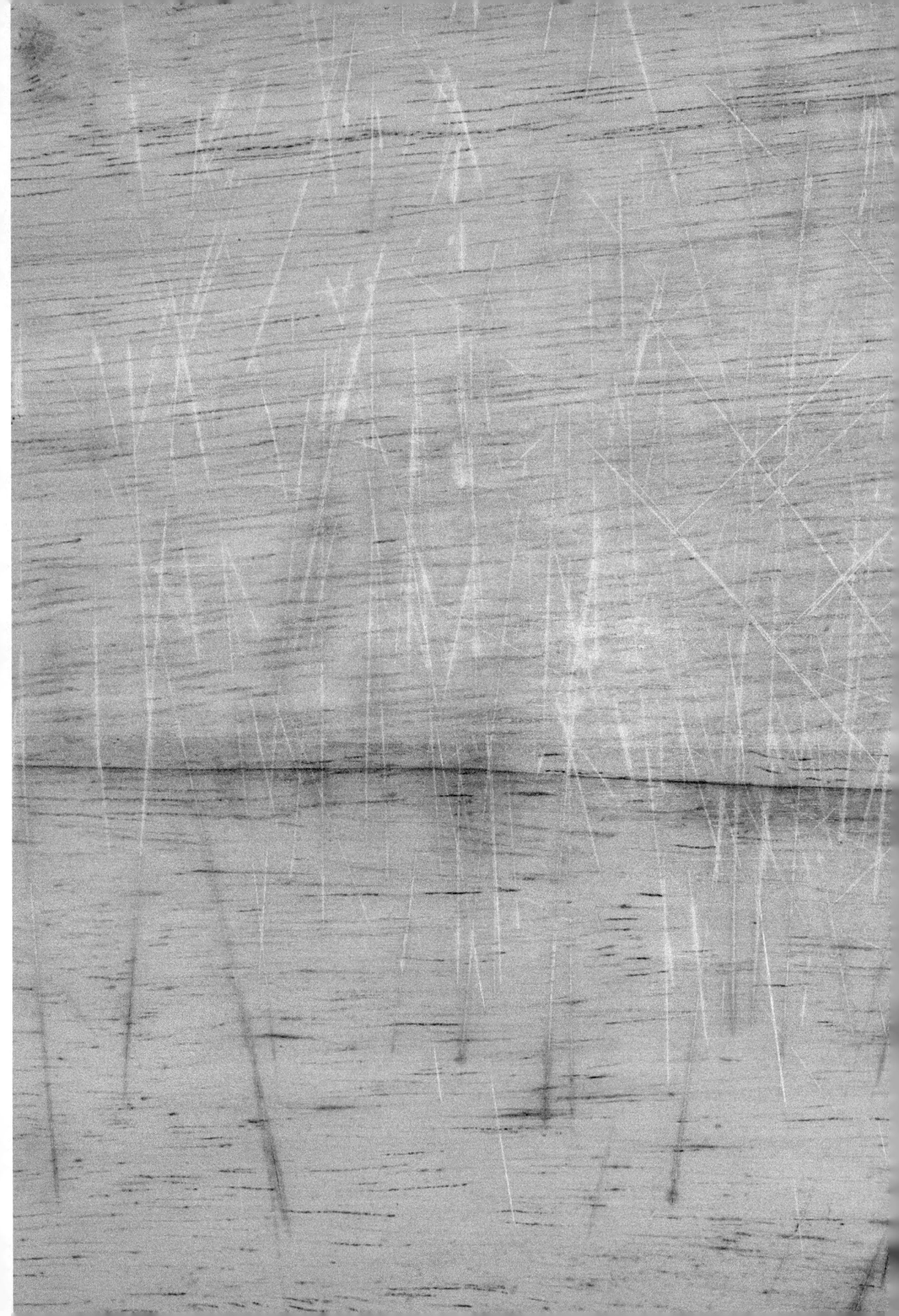

THE COMMUNITY FOOD ASSESSMENT

The food assessment process is a tool by which organizations can determine the need for food services and food information services in their community. Food assessments have the potential to provide all kinds of information that can be used to identify a need, justify a service response, build buy-in and engagement, and plan for the allocation of resources.

In libraries, food assessments create value when considering whether to develop a program series, initiate a new service, or build-out a new space. They can also be used on a larger scale when looking at potential community partnerships or when designing health or food literacy initiatives in partnership with multiple stakeholders such as partner organizations and local government.

There are many ways to conduct an assessment. The approach will depend on the organizations involved, the size and demographics of the community, the purpose and scope of the assessment, and the resources available. This section provides some basic guidelines along with several useful resources to help an organization get started. Complementary worksheets are provided in appendix B, "Tools for the Community Needs Assessment."

Assessing Readiness

Food assessments can be lengthy, complex, and expensive undertakings. It is important to assess readiness before embarking upon the process. Assessing readiness will help organizations determine if they have the necessary resources for an assessment and whether an assessment will move the organization in the right direction.

Here are some questions to ask:

→ **Has a community food assessment been done in your region?**
Previous food and health assessments can provide useful data for your own assessment. You'll want to know what questions have been asked, what trends have been identified, and who the key stakeholders were. Maybe you can build upon the work of a previous assessment and involve those who participated. Check with local health and human services agencies, school districts, and local governments.

→ **Is there community interest in your local food system?**
Specifically, ask the following: Have community members and organizations expressed interest in understanding or changing your local food system? Are there clear issues that your community wants to challenge? Value-driven library service almost always aims to respond to identified community needs. You can find out if this is a topic of interest by attending government meetings, reading local news publications, and reviewing continuing education catalogs and newsletters for local institutes of higher education and community centers.

→ **Has your organization articulated clear questions it wants to pursue via a community food assessment?**
Because you'll want to make the most of your time and money, having clearly defined objectives will be important. These starting objectives will help guide the formation of your planning team and your implementation approach.
It should be noted, however, that questions sometimes change during the planning process and that's OK. The questions you ask may morph based on the stakeholders involved, emergent needs identified in the planning process, and resource allocation guidelines. Be open to this process.

→ **Who are the stakeholders that might be engaged in seeking answers to those questions?**
Would they be willing to commit to serving on a steering committee or planning team? Would the findings of the assessment inform other work these stakeholders are engaged in? Finding stakeholders is an important part of the community food assessment. Consider groups and organizations that you already partner with. Ask them for their ideas on who to involve. Reach out to local governments, school districts, health and food agencies, volunteer service organizations, charitable organizations, and land developers.

CHAPTER 4: THE COMMUNITY FOOD ASSESSMENT 31

➡ **Has your organization identified subject experts to assist with the process?**
A community assessment is a large undertaking. You'll need local residents and employees with expertise to assist with designing, implementing, and facilitating tools such as surveys and focus groups. You'll also need help analyzing community feedback, geographic information system (GIS) maps, and developing visuals—charts and graphs—that share your findings.

➡ **What resources have been identified for possible use in a food assessment?**
Food assessments use time and money, so you'll want to consider which avenues will provide the most support. Have grants been considered? Are key stakeholders or community members able and willing to help with funding? Who would be able and willing to coordinate the food assessment process? Has an outside consultant been considered, and are funds available for this purpose?

➡ **How will the results of the food assessment be shared?**
Don't forget to plan for sharing your results and determining the best way to store your data for future access. Would the assessment be able to inform other work within your community? Is your local government interested in the results? Aside from sharing full results and any final reports with your community and stakeholders, ask local health and government agencies if they would like copies as well.

Getting Started

Most assessments are designed and implemented by a team of employees and stakeholders, so defining and building a team, or steering committee, is often the first step toward this work. It's important to note that the most successful coalitions are formed when a group of stakeholders comes together with a shared need for information—a vested interest. Not only can this result in greater resources, but it can also allow for a more thorough analysis and application of the results. When appointing or inviting members of the team, understanding this buy-in is important, as is clarity around the contribution value. Team members should be vetted to ensure the team includes not only those interested but those with time and skills to contribute.

As a team, begin by asking the following questions: Why are we doing this? What individual values or interests have brought us together? What community issues or questions are we interested to learn more about? What problems need solving? Using these questions as a starting point, the planning team or steering committee can begin to shape the focus of their assessment. The object of initial

Table 4.1 **The community food assessment**

Foundation	Assess readiness
	Build a team
	Determine core questions
	Determine boundaries
Preparation	Determine resources available
	Develop time line
	Create work plan
	Recruit participants
Actualization	Access secondary data and assessments
	Develop research tools
	Conduct research
	Process and analyze data
Evaluation	Summarize and present findings
	Evaluate process
	Celebrate
	Implement follow-up actions

conversations should be to clearly articulate and prioritize one to three core questions that will form the basis of the work.

Something to consider alongside the core questions would be the boundaries of the assessment. These can be political or jurisdictional, such as county lines, cities, and neighborhoods; service designations, including special districts, voting precincts, or census tracks; ethnic/cultural/social; or environmental, using geographical elements as boundaries such as rivers, foothills, or watersheds. When considering the boundaries of an assessment, it will also be important to understand the types of data that are available to help the team study their community. Note that the more granular the boundaries become, the less existing data sets the team will be likely to encounter.

There are two ways to classify the data the team will be encountering and collecting during the assessment:

1. **Primary data** are defined as original data collection obtained through the direct efforts of a researcher or research team. Methods to collect primary

data include surveys and questionnaires, observations, interviews, focus groups, community conversations, and case studies. The advantage of using primary data is that the team would be directly involved in designing the tools and can therefore customize the queries, methods, and objectives. The disadvantages, such as expense, manpower, and skills needed, however, must also be taken into account when opting to collect primary data, as these constraints will often shape the scope of these inquiries.

2. **Secondary data** are defined as data already collected by other groups or individuals, such as other organizations, governmental agencies, and institutes of higher education. The advantage of using secondary data is that obtaining it is usually not expensive and does not require a significant amount of manpower or skill. The main disadvantage is that the data was collected with a specific objective or question in mind, and that question may or may not fully relate to the work the team is doing or address the core questions determined by the stakeholders.

Planning for Success

Once an organization has asked itself the right questions and understands what it hopes to gain from a food assessment, it's time to put together a work plan. A work plan will keep the planners and stakeholders on track toward the identified goals of this large-scale undertaking. As a team embarks on developing their work plan, they should keep in mind two crucial aspects: time line and resources available. In project management speak, these, along with the core questions, or scope, will define the quality of your assessment. The time line, resources available, and core questions should support one other; a change in one will necessitate a change in the others or the quality of the assessment will suffer.

With time line and resources defined and apportioned, the work plan should aim to answer the following questions:

➡ **What?**—What is the specific action or task that needs to be accomplished?
➡ **How?**—How will this be accomplished? What tools or resources will be available for use?
➡ **Who?**—Who will be in charge of ensuring this task is accomplished? Who will support this individual or group?
➡ **When?**—When will this task start, how long is it expected to take, and when is the completion deadline?

The team will want to consider what they already know about their core questions in developing their plan. They should use this knowledge to create a list of the actions that will need to be taken to "get the full picture," or fill the gap between

> ## ESSENTIAL COLLECTIONS
> ### American Road Trip
>
> Because road trips can be journeys of self- and community discovery, I'm including this short list of road-trip-inspired cookbooks, guides, and cultural examinations.
>
> - *Diners, Drive-Ins and Dives: The Funky Finds in Flavortown: America's Classic Joints and Killer Comfort Food.* Fieri, Guy.
> - *Buttermilk Graffiti: A Chef's Journey to Discover America's New Melting-Pot Cuisine.* Lee, Edward.
> - *Eight Flavors: The Untold Story of American Cuisine.* Lohman, Sarah.
> - *Great American Eating Experiences: Local specialties, favorite restaurants, food festivals, diners, roadside stands, and more.* National Geographic.
> - *The American Plate: A Culinary History in 100 Bites.* O'Connell, Libby.
> - *Eating across America: A Foodie's Guide to Food Trucks, Street Food and the Best Dish in Each State.* Patterson, Daymon.
> - *Roadfood, 10th Edition: An Eaters Guide to More than 1,000 of the Best Local Hot Spots and Hidden Gems across America.* Stern, Jane.

what is known and not known about the core questions. The ideal work plan is a living document that begins as a skeletal framework and ends as a fully fleshed-out entity. Successful teams use the plan not only as a step-by-step guideline to the process but for evaluating the whole process, noting what worked and what didn't, what changes were made, what outcomes were expected, and which were unexpected.

A draft work plan will also guide the team in making determinations about the need for participants and experts who will take part in the actualization of the community food assessment. Recruiting volunteers and/or paid staff is an important step that should not be skimped or rushed. When recruiting, you'll want to look for individuals with the following characteristics: detail-oriented, persistent, computer literate, goal-oriented, amiable, fond of people, multilingual, a good and unbiased listener, and observant.[1] Invested participants are good bets—seek within your own organization and those of your partners—but be sure to consider their available time and skills as will be needed by their involvement with the assessment. Other places to seek help include local community colleges, service groups, or like-minded organizations.

Conducting the Assessment

Successful assessments have a few characteristics in common. They start from a strong foundation and a solidly built team. They work with a set of clear values and have established goals for their work. They ask questions that when answered, tell a story and provide community context around an issue. They employ community-based research methods that integrate local organizations and initiatives. They also utilize a well-rounded approach to obtaining existing and new data. To ensure an assessment is well-rounded, it is important to consider asking questions or gathering data from the following sectors of your community's food system: production, transportation and distribution, processing, security and access, policy, economic development, and environmental factors.

When looking for secondary data, or data already collected by other groups and assessments, you'll want to reach out to your local health and human service agencies as well as school districts and local governments. Other sources that could be valuable to this process include the following:

- **American Community Survey** (ACS) data provide detailed information about a political or jurisdictional area's population and housing. Data are released yearly.[2]
- **Community Commons Maps and Data** is a curated collection of data mapping tools, including the CARES Engagement Network, Broadstreet, Win Measures, County Health Rankings and Roadmaps, City Health Dashboard, Policy Map, 500 Cities, and more.[3]
- **Tools from the USDA**, such as the Food Environment Atlas, Food Access Research Atlas, and the Census of Agriculture,[4] allow for targeted GIS mapping and regional analysis of advanced metrics.

When designing research tools to collect primary data, you'll want to keep in mind your options for collecting original data. **Stakeholder interviews** are targeted discussions with individuals selected due to their role within the community. Stakeholders may be business and organization leaders, community activists, community opinion leaders, or even government officials. **Focus groups** are structured interviews of a group of six to twelve people. Participants are typically randomly chosen or chosen from a select group within the larger community. Discussions are facilitated by a moderator operating from a set of preselected questions. A note taker who does not otherwise participate is also usually present to capture the responses. **Community forums** take the focus group approach a step further with a larger audience of participants. Forums are typically composed of a presentation portion and then a hands-on activity or discussion led by a moderator.

Surveys and questionnaires are commonly employed tools for obtaining feedback from large groups of the community. There may be a cost associated with designing the survey tool (if you elect to use a consultation firm) as well as a cost for administering the survey within the community (particularly volunteer time). Surveys can be administered in many ways: pencil and paper at key locations, online via a web form, over the phone, or in person with volunteers and good old-fashioned clipboards. Another source for primary data can be found by conducting **environmental scans**. This tactic relies on observations at key identified locations as well as compiling lists of resources or media within the community.

Here are some additional sources of information about developing your own tools:

- **The USDA Survey Tools** site provides ready-to-use surveys and questionnaires.[5]
- **The Livewell Colorado Data Collection** hosts a wealth of resources from Colorado and beyond. The site shares research tools and full community food assessment plans.[6]
- **The CDC has a Community Needs Assessment guide** that provides step-by-step instructions for designing and implementing an assessment. It is geared toward general community health.[7]
- **The University of Kansas's Community Tool Box** provides a number of tool kits aimed at activities in community work. Their tool kit, Assessing Community Needs and Resources, is particularly helpful.[8]
- **The Community Action Partnership** is another great resource with videos and guides for community-centered work as well as data collection.[9]
- **The Community Food Security Coalition** is a clearinghouse for food assessment guides, tools, and reports.[10]
- **The "What's Cooking in Your Food System?" guide** to community food assessment is one of the best guides available and, incidentally, is often cited in other guides.[11]

Of course, as data are collected via both means—primary and secondary—the team will want to organize the information for easier review and understanding. Coding data simply means to categorize by labeling and grouping. Although it's smart to start with a set of labels or codes that will be used during the processing phase, an intelligent team will reevaluate those codes about midway through to ensure data aren't getting lost due to inadequate classification or grouping. Grouping the data will help you analyze them.

Analysis should be built into the team debrief phase. It should take into account a quantitative and qualitative approach. Quantitative analysis means measuring and comparing numbers. If your question relates to a set of standards, comparing the

CHAPTER 4: THE COMMUNITY FOOD ASSESSMENT 37

community data alongside the standards is a good way to analyze the results. Qualitative analysis may mean building profiles or characteristics lists for comparison or goal setting. Depending on the core assessment questions, both approaches can help the team determine action steps that will close a gap, build a competence, or answer a need in response to the findings.

And Then . . .

It's important to celebrate when the team reaches the conclusion milestone. Months of planning and designing and collecting have paid off and the team now has hundreds of gigabytes and thousands of pages of data.

But again, the work does not stop there because the next steps need to be planned. Whether the team opts to build the action plan themselves or embark on a community planning process, the outcomes—or what is done in support of the data collected from the assessment—should be tied to firm indicators that will help measure the success of any actions implemented as a result.

Some recommended tools for creating action plans and setting indicators are as follows:

- **"Chapter 9: Understanding and Using Your Results"** from *the Community Food Project Evaluation Handbook* explains how to use the data collected from the assessment to build an action plan.[12]
- **On the Community Food Strategies website**, you can find sample assessments and action plans to see how data has been put into action in communities across the country.[13]
- **The University of Wisconsin-Madison's Safe and Healthy Food Pantries Project** has a "Develop Your Action Plan" resource with tips and templates.[14]
- **The American Planning Association** has a knowledge center devoted to food systems planning.[15]

But that's not all, folks. The data must still be summarized and visualized for sharing. Sharing formats might include a written and bound report, an interactive website, or a presentation to the city council or the library board of trustees or even in an open community forum. Whatever the format, the data and findings must be put into a meaningful perspective that can enable the planning team and all stakeholders to clearly see and articulate the next steps.

NOTES

1. "Data Collection and Analysis Guide," USDA Economic Research Service, 2016, www.ers.usda.gov/webdocs/publications/43164/15812_efan02013c_1_.pdf?v=0.

2. "American Community Survey (ACS)," United States Census Bureau, September 26, 2019, www.census.gov/programs-surveys/acs/data.html.
3. "Maps and Data," Community Commons, 2019, www.maps.communitycommons.org.
4. "Food Environment Atlas," USDA, 2019, www.ers.usda.gov/foodatlas/; "Food Access Research Atlas," USDA, 2019, www.ers.usda.gov/data-products/food-access-research-atlas/; "Census of Agriculture," USDA, 2017, www.nass.usda.gov/Publications/AgCensus/2007/.
5. "Survey Tools," USDA, 2019, www.ers.usda.gov/topics/food-nutrition-assistance/food-security-in-the-us/survey-tools/.
6. "Data Collection," Livewell Colorado, 2016, https://livewellcolorado.org/resource-center/research-publication/food-systems/community-food-assessments/data-collection/.
7. "Community Needs Assessment," CDC, 2013, www.cdc.gov/globalhealth/healthprotection/fetp/training_modules/15/community-needs_pw_final_9252013.pdf.
8. University of Kansas, "Assessing Community Needs and Resources," Community Tool Box, 2019, https://ctb.ku.edu/en/assessing-community-needs-and-resources.
9. "ROMA Next Generation," Community Action Partnership, 2019, https://communityactionpartnership.com/results-oriented-management-and-accountability-roma/.
10. "Publications: Newsletters, Views, Handouts, Guidebooks and Reports," Community Food Security Coalition, 2019, http://foodsecurity.org/pubs/.
11. "What's Cooking in Your Food System? A Guide to Community Food Assessment," Community Food Security Coalition, 2002, www.farmlandinfo.org/what%E2%80%99s-cooking-your-food-system-guide-community-food-assessment.
12. *Community Food Project Evaluation Handbook*, National Research Center, 2006, https://nesfp.org/sites/default/files/uploads/cfp_evaluation_handbook.pdf.
13. "Baseline Food System Assessments and Action Plans," Community Food Strategies, 2016, https://communityfoodstrategies.com/what/action/plans/.
14. University of Wisconsin-Madison, "Develop Your Action Plan," Safe and Healthy Food Pantries Project, 2019, https://fyi.extension.wisc.edu/safehealthypantries/action-plan/.
15. "Food Systems," APA, KnowledgeBase Collection, 2019, www.planning.org/knowledgebase/food/.

FOOD LITERACY QUICK-START GUIDE

Whether or not your library has opted to pursue a community food assessment, planning a food literacy program or service should still be put through the rigors of any in-house design and evaluation process. The policies and processes libraries have developed serve two key roles within overall program development: first, they set standards and expectations for the quality and value of the library's offerings, and second, they ensure responsible and thoughtful use of taxpayer funds.

That being said, there are certainly times to challenge the norms. If your library has a strict *no-food* policy, it may be time to revisit the in-house design and evaluation process. For libraries where adding food or heat to the menu would be a huge leap, consider a community food assessment to aid in the process of justifying the new service response.

If your library doesn't have a design and evaluation process, ask yourself the following questions:

- Does the idea meet a strategic goal? Does it serve the library's mission?
- Is there an interest in the idea from the community? Does it meet a community need or demand?
- Would this have an impact on staff and their day-to-day work? How much? Is the added value of the idea worth it?
- Does support for the idea exist within the community? The staff? Library stakeholders?
- Are any associated risks possible to mediate or overcome?

➡ Does the library have the resources to implement the idea? Can the resources be found?

A library able to answer "yes" to most of these questions is in a good position to get started. Other questions that programmers may want to ask prior to embarking on a new program or service would include questions of time line, how success would be measured, as well as whether the program would need to be sustainable.

Program Logistics

When planning a food program, you'll need to consider things you may not have put much thought into before with other run-of-the-mill library programs or storytimes:

➡ **How many people should we plan for?**
If your program is hands-on, you'll want some wiggle room. Just because a room seats fifty doesn't mean that will work for a cooking class or *Iron Chef* contest. You'll want space for participants to move around their workspaces, equipment, and each other. You'll also need space for waste and composting bins, cleaning supplies, and emergency gear such as a first aid station.

➡ **What about my meeting room?**
Take a look at the space the program will be utilizing and review the use policies related to those spaces. Is the lighting adequate? Is there enough room for your setup? Is there enough ventilation? What equipment do you have (or can you use)? Is there a sink? Will cooking set off a fire alarm? If you're unsure about the use of heat or open flames or other cooking equipment, consult with your facilities team or your fire marshal.

➡ **Do we need to know about food safety and sanitation?**
A good food program will inform and practice good food safety. Depending on the scale of your program, this may mean a reminder to wash hands and having gloves on hand, or it may mean that your staff need to be certified in food handling. ServSafe is one of the best-known food safety certification programs in the country; the Food Handler online course and exam fee is $15 per participant. The program and materials are offered in English and Spanish. Another option is to go through your local state extension office.

➡ **What about general safety and waivers?**
If you're going to use knives, be sure to first demonstrate the ways to hold and handle a knife. Don't assume everyone knows this! If you are going to offer a series of hands-on cooking or food prep programs, start with knife skills. When

ENGAGING FOODIE WEBSITES AND APPS FOR KIDS

Eat & Move-O-Matic by Learning Games Lab, New Mexico State University.
A hands-on tool to help children understand the role foods play in energy use. Calorie consumption is also broken down using a simple "if you eat x, you can burn it off by doing y" algorithm.

Fizzy's Lunch Lab by PBS. www.pbskids.org/lunchlab.
Recommended for ages four and up, this interactive website promotes good nutrition and exercise through fun games, delicious and easy-to-make recipes, dance- and jump-along videos, printable place mats, and more. There's also an app called Fizzy's Lunch Lab: Fresh Pick, which is free and includes further activities such as math skills, reasoning, and basic operations.

FreeRice. www.beta.freerice.com.
Recommended for ages eight and up, children will learn about world hunger and contribute to the solution by answering trivia questions. For each question answered correctly, the United Nations World Food Programme will donate ten grains of rice to a community in need.

Issa's Edible Adventures. https://issasedibleadventures.com.
This free app for children ages six and up follows Issa on her adventures around the globe. Work with Issa in the kitchen to learn about special cultural meals as well as global and socially conscious foods.

This Is My Food—Nutrition for Kids by urbn pockets.
http://urbnpockets.com/apps/this-is-my-food-nutrition-for-kids/show.
This STEM app focuses on nutrition for kids. Its colorful and easy-to-navigate format will appeal to children as young as four years old. Learn about food classifications, eating behaviors, and food from around the world. Also, there is a fun printable guide available on the developer's website.

Toca Kitchen by Toca Boca. www.tocaboca.com/app/toca-kitchen-2/.
Toca Boca has based all their wildly popular children's apps on the concept of play. And what's more fun than playing with your food? In this fun app for ages two and up, choose between a handful of fun characters and then get to work in the kitchen prepping food that will delight or disgust.

Yummiloo. www.yummico.com/yummiloo.
This app is accessible for children as young as two years old. It uses color matching as the basis for helping children learn to be curious about vegetables and introduces the concept of composting.

ESSENTIAL COLLECTIONS
Cooking with Kids

The following selection provides a variety of cookbooks for kids. Most of these books go a step further by providing specific technique instruction as well as background information to a cooking style or particular type of food. But cookbooks are being released all the time. Some things to look for in top-notch cookbooks for kids are as follows: use of professional terms with a glossary, step-by-step instructions (even better with photos or illustrations), ingredient or tool tips for first-time users, and a guide to measurements and conversions.

- *The Complete Cookbook for Young Chefs*. America's Test Kitchen.
- *Baking with Kids*. Brooks, Leah.
- *The Young Chef: Recipes and Techniques for Kids Who Love to Cook*. Culinary Institute of America.
- *A Smart Girl's Guide: Cooking: How to Make Food for Your Friends, Your Family and Yourself*. Daniels, Patricia et al.
- *The Nourishing Traditions Cookbook for Children: Teaching Children to Cook the Nourishing Traditions Way*. Gross, Suzanne et al.
- *Kid Chef: The Foodie Kids Cookbook: Healthy Recipes and Culinary Skills for the New Cook in the Kitchen*. Hammer, Melina.
- *Mom and Me Cookbook*. Karmel, Annabel.
- *The Toddler Cookbook*. Karmel, Annabel.
- *Honest Pretzels: And 64 Other Amazing Recipes for Cooks Ages 8 and Up*. Katzen, Mollie.
- *Pretend Soup and Other Real Recipes: A Cookbook for Preschoolers and Up*. Katzen, Mollie.
- *MasterChef Junior Cookbook: Bold Recipes and Essential Techniques to Inspire Young Cooks*. McLachlan, Clay.
- *Eat Your Greens, Reds, Yellows, and Purples: Children's Cookbook*. Mitchem, James, Love, Carrie, and King, Dave.
- *The Help Yourself Cookbook for Kids: 60 Easy Plant-Based Recipes Kids Can Make to Stay Healthy and Save the Earth*. Roth, Ruby.
- *The Silver Spoon for Children: Favorite Italian Recipes*. Russell, Harriet, and Grant, Amanda.
- *The Tickle Fingers Toddler Cookbook: Hands-On Fun in the Kitchen for 1 To 4s*. Woolmer, Annabel.

it comes to heat and open flame, ask participants to tie back their hair and avoid loose and baggy clothing and accessories. Keep a fully equipped first aid kit nearby and make sure staff know the procedures for handling a cut, burn, or other safety mishap. Waivers are generally a good idea when working with knives and heat.

➡ **Can kids use knives?**
This is a common concern. In our craft programs, we will often relegate paper cutters and glue guns to adult staff or volunteers, so the question naturally follows, how much can we really do with kids? Learning kitchen safety such as basic knife skills and how to be safe around a hot surface are important lessons to learn. It will be up to the individual library to make the determination for themselves about their comfort level around this issue. But there are work-arounds and alternate plans you can make if you want to avoid knives in kid's hands. There are kid-safe nylon or safety knives such as the Opinel Le Petit Chef Knife, the Kuhn Rikon Doggy Knife, or the Curious Chef Nylon Knife Set.

How Do We Deal with Food Allergies?
The best practice is to be overly informative about the food that will be used in your program. Print clear labels and include allergens in your waiver document. Train staff to recognize the symptoms of an allergic reaction and make sure they know how to respond to a possible allergic reaction.

How Can We Get the Food?
Depending on the scale of your program, you can either purchase items yourself from a local grocer or, better yet, invite the grocer to be a partner and donate the food. For larger programs and series, consider working with a food distributor like US Foods, which will allow you to place bulk orders online and receive deliveries at your location. There are a lot of benefits from working with a distributor—they will often have training materials and discounts on bulk purchasing and can make referrals to other services that may be needed for larger-scale programs and teaching kitchens.

How Do We Know What Kitchen Equipment to Purchase?
There are a number of valuable guides available online, including on the websites of online retailers, but you could also ask local restaurants where they purchase their equipment. Many restaurant supply companies also offer a consultation and equipment spec service. Additionally, if you are looking to go big, consider hiring a kitchen consultant to help you plan your space and help with any permits or certifications needed in your state.

How Do We Circulate That?

When building a special circulating collection, such as cake pans or food thermometers, you will definitely need to consider sustainability. At some point—whether they are lost, damaged, or wear out—those items will need to be replaced. Will the library make a commitment to support this collection in the long term? If so, you'll also need a procedure for processing and circulating those items. This may even necessitate an additional clause in the collection development policy if the current policy doesn't provide for such a scenario. Some additional considerations: you won't be able to stick a barcode on items that will go in an oven or sink, and you'll want to set expectations for the cleanliness of a returned item.

The questions earlier (and probably more) will end up on your plate when you go the route of providing a food literacy program or service to your community. But don't let the uncertainty of the unknown cool your enthusiasm. Today makerspaces are fairly common in libraries across the country, but you can bet that the first few were built with a certain trepidation alongside the excitement of providing a new service to the community.

PART III

"THE PROOF IS IN THE PUDDING"

SHORT ORDERS

Since libraries began offering programs to the public, they've known that the best way to get started with a new topic is to simply give it a try. This section will highlight programs and services of small to medium scope. Many of these were one-off events, meaning they were single events that stood on their own and weren't necessarily part of a broader initiative. In all cases, the libraries featured were answering a need within their communities and weren't afraid to get sticky.

BACKYARD CHICKEN BASICS

The next example, from the Parker Memorial Library in Dracut, Massachusetts, is one of many agriculture and husbandry library programs that are quickly gaining traction around the country. Animals have made appearances in libraries before—with alpacas and snakes coming for a visit from local farms and zoos— but what makes this program stand out is the Parker Memorial staff's agility and willingness to hear a community problem and engineer a clever community-based solution.

By Diane Annunziato

Dracut, Massachusetts, is anchored by its heritage as a farming community. A recent designation as a "right-to-farm community" via vote at a town meeting reignited the simmering interest of many residents to go back to Dracut's roots by planting residential gardens of all sizes and exploring the various aspects of animal husbandry.

Many homes began to support horses, goats, and flocks of chickens. The Parker Memorial Library experienced numerous requests for information on gardening, beekeeping, and animal husbandry. Requests for information on acquiring and raising chickens were overwhelming. Our children's librarian, herself a farmer, seldom had a week pass without at least one direct request for information regarding the care and raising of chickens.

As a result of the reference interviews conducted with patrons seeking information about raising backyard chickens, we realized that there was a lot of misinformation circulating. This included complaints from sleepless residents looking for information regarding the right-to-farm bylaws, who were hoping that there was a restriction on the number of roosters allowed. (Contrary to popular belief, roosters crow throughout the night, not just at sunrise, and it is not necessary to have a rooster in the flock for successful egg production.)

To serve the increasing demand for information, we had been steadily increasing our available resources by purchasing books, instructional DVDs, and so on regarding all aspects of gardening, beekeeping and animal husbandry, bookmarking and publicizing information on databases, and offering programs addressing the most sought-after topics. One such topic was the acquisition, raising, and sustained care of producing chicken flocks.

A search for a presenter for a primer on raising chickens resulted in the discovery of Tom Doherty, a well-qualified expert from the Aviculture Exchange in Westford, Massachusetts. (Tom is known as "Westford's Chicken Man.") Sponsored by the Dracut Agricultural Commission, the program was titled Backyard Chicken Basics and featured Tom's presentation, with a Dracut animal control officer present to participate in the after-program patron Q&A. We publicized the program in-house, at other town buildings, online, on local community television, in local papers, and through social media, flyers and sandwich boards. A prominent display in our library lobby featured our available materials, handouts featuring other resources and our upcoming Backyard Chicken Basics program. Overwhelmingly successful, our meeting room was filled to capacity with more than sixty people attending.

The results of this program were far reaching. The number of successful chicken flocks increased, with happy patrons regularly reporting to us on their progress. Fewer roosters were acquired and some who previously had roosters, realizing that they didn't need them, rehomed them elsewhere much to the relief of their neighbors. Inspired by this program and the resources available from the library, the Agricultural Commission, and the Aviculture Exchange, several local schools acquired incubators and instituted hatching programs to the delight of parents and students. Patrons requested more programs in keeping with the community's farming history, food, and cooking.

In response to the numerous requests for more programming in this vein, the staff of the Parker Memorial Library chose the theme "Dracut Reads and Eats 2018!" for the next community-wide read. Over a period of two months, more than thirty programs focusing on the agricultural roots of the community featured all aspects of farming, cooking, and food. This included programming for adults, teens, and children.

Four books were featured as the main course, including *Clearing Land: Legacies of an American Farm* by Jane Brox. Jane grew up on a farm (still existing) in Dracut. This is the third of three books about the Brox Farm and its history. In addition, a featured program included a cooking demonstration of classic Korean dishes, which were prepared and served in classic bronze ware (*bangjja*) by Korean chefs dressed in traditional clothing. Afterward, a short film on Korean history was presented. Seventeen local restaurants participated in the community-wide program by offering substantial discounts to any patron who displayed their "Dracut Reads and Eats 2018!" button.

As a result of Dracut Reads and Eats 2018!, there was an increased interest and participation in local community-supported agriculture (CSA) sites, in eating local (both in farm produce and restaurants), in cooking, and in the history of Dracut. We have had many requests for more programming about the culture and food of other countries. At this time, we are considering a year of programming that would feature a different country's culture and cooking quarterly. We haven't yet reached the end of the actual outcomes from Backyard Chicken Basics!

INTERNATIONAL EDIBLE BOOK DAY

Nothing brings folks to libraries quicker than announcing there will be food. Now imagine if the books were made from food. That's exactly the premise of International Edible Books Day—a day when readers are encouraged to share their love of books by creating edible facsimiles with artistic flair. At Saint Mary's Hall in San Antonio, Texas, a partnership between a teacher and a librarian created this program to bring the students and teachers together in an artistic and educational activity.

By Linda Plevak

International Edible Book Day was an annual celebration for many years when I was the middle school / upper school librarian at Saint Mary's Hall, a private school in San Antonio, Texas. The program sprang from a partnership with Carol Parker-Mittal, teacher of fine arts, when she told me about the concept of edible books. Dreamed up by librarian and activist Judith Hoffberg and artist Beatrice Coron, Edible Books Day began in 2000. Looking at photos of cakes and other edibles inspired by books, we both agreed to give it a try.

To start, we contacted several other teachers at the school, and we all agreed it was a great idea for collaboration for the upper school. Our goal was to host an

TIPS FOR HOSTING YOUR OWN EDIBLE BOOK DAY

- Create a rubric or a simple spreadsheet with a Likert scale for each category for the judges to use when scoring the entries.
- Invite a backup judge, just in case someone cancels.
- Make sure the entries are numbered with no names so judging is fair.
- Have other food and drinks (a must!) available. This gives attendees and participants something to chew on while the judges make their decisions. It also provides something to eat besides the entries.
- Make sure refrigeration and possibly a freezer are available for entries, especially if the competition is held after school. In the entry form, include a space for requesting refrigeration or a freezer.
- Include international students by encouraging competitors to represent foreign literature.
- Ask participants to list ingredients for those sampling their creations. This will help those with food allergies and/or dietary enjoy the celebration.

event that would bring students, faculty, and staff together in the library. Students would use problem-solving and critical-thinking skills. Their creations would require them to think creatively in the following academic areas: art, literature, culinary arts, and biology/nutrition.

As the librarian, I assembled a small team of teachers and staff to plan logistics and to promote our Edible Book Day (EBD). In preparation, we designed posters and flyers to advertise International Edible Book Day throughout campus. We included the prize categories and the official EBD website for inspiration. Personal invites were sent to each teacher to encourage their participation and the inclusion of their students. We created a special book display of classic literature and food. Some were fiction that included food and recipes. Others were literary-themed cookbooks. We included flyers and a copy of the guidelines with the book display.

The planning team decided that we would host two competitions: one for students and another for faculty and staff. The participants would be eligible to win prizes for their creations in the following categories: most creative, most aesthetically pleasing, most delicious, best theme, most nutritious, and best pun. We solicited prizes and gift cards from local businesses. We recruited judges (one student, two teachers, one staff). We asked students to sign up if they planned to enter to ensure that we would have entries and also to encourage other students to join in. We set a deadline for entering but also stated that they could enter at the event.

Here are a few of the guidelines we shared in the promotional materials:

- Entry must be a book or book theme.
- All the parts of your entry *must be edible*!
- Keep it clean and appropriate (just a good reminder).

Our first International Edible Book Day was a great success! Both students and staff enthusiastically participated, and prizes were awarded in all the categories. Many other students and staff came to see and cheer on their friends. We decided it was an event worth repeating. The second year was even better with more participants because students and staff knew about Edible Book Day from the previous year. And so it was decided that Edible Book Day would become an annual tradition that was enjoyed for many years afterward.

International Edible Book Day brings together visual arts, nutrition, culinary arts, and, of course, literature! Although we held our event before the days of social media, in my opinion, this event is just ready to be gobbled up by followers on your library's Instagram feed! Bon appétit!

ESSENTIAL COLLECTIONS
Travel Memoir and World Food Culture

Reading about food can be almost as nice as eating it. In this collection of memoirs and cultural explorations, readers can have the armchair traveler experience at its best.

- *A Moveable Feast.* Bourdain, Anthony.
- *Food Lover's Guide to the World: Experience the Great Global Cuisines.* Bain, Carolyn.
- *Try This: Traveling the Globe without Leaving the Table.* Freeman, Danyelle.
- *Eating Words: A Norton Anthology of Food Writing.* Gilbert, Sandra et al.
- *Let the Meatballs Rest: And Other Stories about Food and Culture.* Montanari, Massimo.
- *Food Journeys of a Lifetime: 500 Extraordinary Places to Eat around the Globe.* National Geographic.
- *A Fork in the Road: Tales of Food, Pleasure and Discovery on the Road.* Oseland, James.
- *The World Atlas of Street Food.* Quinn, Sue.
- *Save Me the Plums.* Reichl, Ruth.
- *1,000 Foods to Eat before You Die: A Food Lover's Life List.* Sheraton, Mimi.

CUPCAKE WARS

Many of our patrons (and ourselves) have indulged in a binge watch of a popular cooking television show—especially competitions like Chopped, Hell's Kitchen, or The Great British Bake Off. What better way to take that enthusiasm and interest to the next level by offering a food competition of our own? At the Tenafly Public Library in New Jersey, inspired by the popularity of cooking shows and the aspirations of two local bakeries, librarians designed a program that allowed patrons to join in the fun.

By Latricia Markle

By the summer of 2016, two local bakeries had competed on the Food Network show *Cupcake Wars* and another local bakery ran an always-full cake camp every summer. Adults were talking about the TV show and some showed off pictures of cakes they attempted for this party or that event. This left us with little doubt that the kids in our community loved to play with their food and adults were also interested in decorating. We were looking for a program that could work for whole families, multiple generations, and children of many different ability levels.

Our vision was having family members and friends register as teams (three to five members per team with at least one person over 13 years of age), each team choosing a book or literary character to inspire the decoration of three cupcakes. In the middle of the competition, we would have teams draw a "twist" from a hat. Our twists included the following: "One member of the team can talk but not touch the cupcakes. Another member of the team can touch the cupcakes but can't talk," "Two members must work with their ankles tied together," "You have lost the use of your utensils; hands only from here on out," and others. This added a zany element to our competition that would be fun to watch.

We scheduled the program in the middle of our summer reading program and started the buzz early because we were worried about getting enough families interested. During school visits in June, we told the kids about it. We sent flyers to the home school academies and to parents we knew were active in PASET (Parents Association for Special Education in Tenafly); we also posted on our social media accounts and included the flyer in all summer reading press releases.

At the beginning of the summer, we hoped for eight to ten teams for the event. Members of our Friends of the Library group volunteered to be judges and planned to use this event to promote their fall fundraiser, an Edible Book Festival. We bought cupcake charms for the winning team. Our youth services staff as well as some adult services staff pitched in to prep for the program. Staff members volunteered to bake cupcakes and make royal icing. We planned to buy canned frosting and *lots* of candy and cereal for decoration fodder.

Then the registrations started rolling in . . . and in . . . and in. A week before the program, we had twenty teams registered with a total of more than seventy individuals. This probably isn't a huge program for some libraries, but we are a small- to midsized library, and our programs averaged twenty to thirty people with the occasional one hundred plus for events such as puppet shows or magicians. This one blew our expectations out of the water. We recruited more staff members to bake, and more teens were asked to volunteer to help set up and help at the event.

We baked more than six dozen cupcakes and made four batches of royal icing. We bought cereal, candy, sprinkles, food coloring, candy eyes, chips, pretzels, and anything else we could think of that would work for decoration. We avoided all nut products. We borrowed tables from our recreation department and set up twenty-two tables for registered teams (and two last-minute registrations) and five tables of supplies.

On the day of the event, there were two no-shows and one surprise show. The teams were diverse: a parent with their child and two young friends, four tweens, a dad and his autistic teenaged daughter and ten-year-old twins. Our teen volunteers handed out three cupcakes per team, paper plates, paper bowls, and plastic knives. After reviewing the rules, once time started, they had an hour to decorate their cupcakes. There was no stealing candy, no hoarding candy, and no eating your cupcakes until *after* judging, but eating some candy was allowed (and encouraged). We asked the teams to get supplies in shifts to avoid a stampede.

This program exceeded expectations. It remains one of our most well-attended events *ever*. While most of the attendees were under the age of ten, we did have a significant number of parents who participated and that were also spectators. Kids as young as five and teens as old as fourteen were active members of teams, and all the feedback was positive. We have done this two more times as a teen-only program and once more as an all-ages program. These are run essentially the same way but have been smaller. We are planning to cave in to the requests for another family/kids Cupcake War this summer—galaxy of cupcakes, here we come!

GETTING STARTED WITH YOUR INSTANT POT

When e-readers first appeared on the market, libraries were inundated with patrons every January, bringing their new devices in to ask our help. As new kitchen appliances hit the market, patrons likewise pop in to see what books we have to help them figure out their new toys. The Holmes County District Public Library listened to their patrons' requests and went a step further by offering a hands-on experience to help them learn.

By Christina Thurairatnam

The Instant Pot became a big sensation in 2017 and a lot of people in our area received them as Christmas gifts. I started purchasing Instant Pot cookbooks for our collection when I noticed the trend and that the books were flying off the shelves. Two of my coworkers had received or purchased Instant Pots around the holidays, and while one of them had tried a few things, the other one was so nervous about using it that she hadn't even taken it out of the box yet. I did some casual research and realized that a lot of people felt the same way about starting to cook with the Instant Pot. I decided that I wanted to have some kind of program on cooking with the Instant Pot and other similar multicookers.

My main issue was that I didn't have an Instant Pot, and I barely know how to use a slow cooker, so I couldn't teach the class myself. After I saw a post in a library programming group about a library that had presenters teach the class, I realized that I could check with my county extension office and ask if they could present the program. While my extension office representative didn't have an Instant Pot, she knew someone in a neighboring county extension office that had presented a program with the Instant Pot, so they were able to collaborate on the program together.

The program ended up being led by the Ohio State University Extension Office in Holmes County, Ohio. They are a branch of OSU that connects with the community, and they present educational programs and distribute publications. One of their foci is family and consumer science, so they have educators who can teach classes on cooking and nutrition. A lot of states have similar extension offices.

We decided to hold the program on a Tuesday evening. I let the presenters know our budget and they came up with a menu and purchased the ingredients, which we then reimbursed. The presenters made hard-cooked eggs, beef stew, and molten chocolate cakes. The only costs associated with the program were the ingredients and the mileage for the out-of-county extension office representative. The program was advertised in our events page newsletter, in the library, on our website and Facebook page, and in the newspaper.

My expectations for the program were that we'd have a decent-size class, maybe twelve people, and that they would leave the class feeling more prepared to use their Instant Pot or multicooker. In the past, I hadn't had the best attendance at educational programs. The actual outcome was that our registration filled up quickly and we had to add a waiting list. We had twenty-three people in attendance. While I didn't do a formal survey, I did get positive verbal feedback from some of the attendees. I think the program was a success, and it was relatively easy to put together. Our Instant Pot cookbooks are just as popular as ever, and I have contacted our extension office about doing another cooking class later this year.

CAKE DECORATING FOR TEENS

The Shaker Heights Public Library in Ohio was looking for a way to help teens learn more about potential careers in the culinary arts. For teens who used public transit, allowing them to learn at their local library was a must. Library staff partnered with a local bakery to help bring a taste of the baking life to their teens.

By Audrey L. Jacobs

Following our simple hands-on food programs, making *pudding dirt cups* and *walking tacos*, our library's teens were pouring over cookbooks from the young adults (YA) collection. Students began to talk about what they cooked at home. They were actually baking, just desserts, mostly from boxed mixes. Some boasted that their results were so good they could become chefs someday. The possibility of making those dreams a reality for these students had recently increased because of new affordable culinary arts certificate programs at our local community college. It was time for a real-world experience.

When planning for this program, it was important to keep everything local because our teens were very neighborhood oriented and only used public transportation. The community college couldn't help us unless we could bring the teens to them—which we couldn't do. Considering other potential partners led to Lucy's Sweet Surrender, an old-world European style bakery that had just relocated to our neighborhood. Owner Michael Feigenbaum quickly agreed to come to both our main and branch locations to do two cake decorating programs with teens. He would take care of everything.

My hope was for these programs to introduce students to the relationship between their interests and potential careers. I also wanted them to experience the power and joy of succeeding at something new. Finding out about something that wasn't even on their radar, which goes on every day in their own neighborhood, would be a bonus. The young men mostly talked about coming for the food and the young women about making roses out of icing. Along with the posturing, I could see the physical manifestations of intense pride radiating from the group afterward. It was a young man, who surprised me, by quietly approaching the baker after the program to ask if he could come hang out at the bakery to learn more about it.

DIA DE LOS MUERTOS COMMUNITY ALTAR

Helping participants connect with their community through cultural values is what sets this program apart from many food literacy programs. At the Gwinnett County Public Library in Lawrenceville, GA, library staff sought to create a meaningful program through local partnerships.

Jené Watson, interviewed

For two consecutive years, Ms. Watson has maintained a community partnership with a local group named Dichos de la Casa to bring Dia de los Muertos programs to the Gwinnett County Public Library patrons. Dichos de la Casa is a local organization, founded by scholar and food activist Karla Blaginin in an effort to create and share educational presentations to share with various sectors of the public. Dichos works with local families and groups in the Latin community in the creation of their programs and presentations.

Ms. Watson first heard about the work of Dichos through a colleague who had learned about a Mexican fruit cup program at the local schools, a direct product of Dichos de la Casa. Karla Blaginin was contacted, and the first program offered at the library was a salsa-making demonstration.

Following soon after that, Ms. Watson and Ms. Blaginin began to plan for the Dia de los Muertos Community Altar program. In this program, participants learned about the important place that aromatic food plays in the building and setting of *ofrendas*, or remembrance altars. Traditional foods, such as *tamales, champurrado*, and *pan de muerto*, were also discussed and sampled. Additionally, the program included a lecture and hands-on craft activity.

The library brands their collaborations with Dichos de la Casa as youth and family programs. The goal is to create ways for library patrons—especially children and teens—to experience more closely traditions with which they may have little or passing familiarity. The library also wanted to be inclusive of their Latin American heritage patrons, allowing them to see themselves and their values in the library's services. Forging connections between North American and Mexican traditions allowed patrons to see and talk about similarities between ancestral remembrance traditions.

Ms. Watson's part of the preparation involved creating the general program plan, coordinating the planning sessions with Karla and the community groups that she identified as potential partners, initiating e-mail communication between the organizers, curating books and relevant materials from the collection, securing space for the program, purchasing supplemental supplies as needed, creating promotional materials, and then stepping out of the way so that Karla and the youth presenters could share their culture with the audience in an authentic way.

The outcomes were aligned with the library's mission and patrons of both Latin heritage and other ethnic backgrounds were drawn in. Patron feedback was positive, many attendees took the time to thank the planners for putting it together. Some identified that the program helped dispel myths and misconceptions about Dia de los Muertos. Others shared that they were happy to see that kind of cultural celebration happening in their library. The success of the Dia programs has led to other food-based program collaborations with Dichos de la Casa at the Gwinnett County Public Library, such as Experience Kimchi! Science in a Korean Mother's Kitchen and My Mexican Mother's Kitchen.

DEATH BY CHOCOLATE

Who doesn't love chocolate? In this innovative program, the library sought to draw in patrons with a sweet tooth by tempting them with chocolate. At the Clermont County Public Library in Ohio, library staff wanted patrons to enjoy a storytelling experience while digging into a popular topic to explore the history behind one of our favorite sweets.

By Lisa Breithaupt

I have done a chocolate program for many years at the Clermont County Public Library. When I designed the program, I did so because who doesn't love chocolate? Cookbooks always circulate well, especially dessert cookbooks. And besides, food programs always interest our patrons.

I did a lot of research regarding the history of chocolate, and I did a lot of reading related to the subject so I could booktalk them throughout the program. I also worked on a personal story. I am a storyteller, and I belong to the Dreamweavers storytelling troupe. We perpetuate the art of the oral tradition, and I worked on a personal story involving my granny and her recipe for chocolate gravy (a hot chocolate pudding that she served on top of our biscuits). I also researched various chocolate bars and the dates in which they were invented and some of the stories behind the names, conceptualization, history of the chocolate bars.

I had a partner when doing the program, and we took turns speaking during the course of the program. We decided to make a simple snack for our attendees based on the chocolate-covered potato chips that are sold at Neiman Marcus at $22.00 for 10 ounces. We simply used Ruffles potato chips and a bag of semisweet chocolate

---

DEATH BY CHOCOLATE

Rich, Dark, Sweet, ummmmm. We all love chocolate. The Taste, the Smell, the mere sight of it. Join us at the Library as we tantalize our senses with chocolate. We'll discuss the history of chocolate, chocolate trivia, chocolate in literature, chocolate recipes and we'll be sure to taste some as well. This program is not for you if you are on the Adkins diet . . . but if you cheat it will be our secret.

(Marketing copy form the Clermont County Public Library, Ohio)

CHOCOLATE-THEMED FICTION BOOKLIST

- *Chocolate for a Woman's Blessing.* Allenbaugh, Kay.
- *French Silk.* Brown, Sandra.
- *Chocolate Puppy Puzzle: A Chocoholic Mystery.* Carl, Joanna.
- *Beyond the Chocolate War.* Cormier, Robert.
- *The Chocolate War.* Cormier, Robert.
- *Blood and Chocolate.* Curtis Klause, Annette.
- *Of Course You Know That Chocolate Is a Vegetable and Other Stories.* D'Amato, Barbara.
- *The Madhatter's Guide to Chocolate.* Devane, Rhett.
- *Like Water for Chocolate.* Esquivel, Laura.
- *Such Devoted Sisters.* Goudge, Eileen.
- *Chocolat.* Harris, Joanne.
- *Chocolate Cat Caper.* Hyde, Elisabeth.
- *Chocolate Chip Cookie Murder.* Hyde, Elisabeth.
- *Chocolate Frog Frame Up.* Hyde, Elisabeth.
- *Crazy as Chocolate.* Hyde, Elisabeth.
- *Death by Chocolate.* McKevett, G. A.
- *Dying for Chocolate.* Mott Davidson, Diana.
- *Death Is Semi-Sweet.* Temple, Lou.

chips found at any supermarket. We microwaved the chocolate until melted and smooth and drizzled them on to the chips, which we laid out in a single layer on a cookie sheet. After a few minutes the chocolate set, and we had a simple, inexpensive, easy treat for any occasion.

We tackled the topic of chocolate in a few entertaining ways. We discussed the history and trivia of chocolate and asked the audience chocolate trivia. The winner received a "kiss"—chocolate, of course. We made simple chocolate treats to be enjoyed by the audience during the program. We also inserted mini booktalks through the program on books with the theme of chocolate. We concluded with a chocolate taste test, which, not surprisingly, was the most popular. For this activity, we purchased different brands and varieties of chocolate and offered samples. The audience voted on which ones they liked best at the end.

RAMEN IRON CHEF

Playing with your food can be a fun way to explore new combinations and flavors. When the Columbus Public Library of the Chattahoochee Valley Libraries in Georgia brought ramen to the table, teens had a blast.

By Megan Aarant

I hosted a program called Ramen Iron Chef where I provided teens with ingredients to create an "entrée" ramen noodle dish and a "dessert" ramen noodle dish. I precooked the ramen noodles (without the spices) and portioned them out on plates. Teens got to take two plates; one for each dish. Ingredients included fresh vegetables, seaweed sheets, cheese, hot dogs, spices, hot sauce, soy sauce, candy, chocolate sauce, Oreos, vanilla wafers, whipped cream, and licorice. I also had some Japanese candies and snacks for them to eat and use as ingredients as well.

I gave them forty-five minutes to work individually or in teams to create a dish. It could be serious, or it could be a crazy gross-out dish. Then I brought staff members over to tour the treats. Several staff members informally voted on their own to award someone a creative use of treats prize but that wasn't originally part of the program. And afterward, because they are teens, almost all the plates of ramen were eaten. Most of them on dares because they did not look particularly appetizing . . . ha ha!

I originally identified the need for this program because I knew that the teens liked to get messy and creative, eat food, and were into Japanese culture. I hosted an otaku club where teens watched anime, talked manga, and played card games, with every other meeting adding an activity. Ramen Iron Chef was one of those activities.

I prepared by searching Pinterest to see how other libraries had handled *Iron Chef*-type programs and saw that some had done so with ramen. I decided to buy precut, prewashed vegetables and items that were individually wrapped to save time and for safety considerations, so we didn't have to have a lot of knives out for cutting. I covered the tables in butcher paper and drew out sections for each team to place their plates in. The teens then took markers and decorated their teams' section.

I expected the teens to have fun and for it to be messy. This did happen, but I didn't realize how creative they would get or how into it they would be. During the staff tour of treats, two teens performed a five-minute impromptu rap about their entrée and dessert, which was quite impressive. They were able to name their dish, explain the concept, tell us why we should eat it, and why Japan is cool. I also expected the teens to learn a little bit more about how to create a dish from seemingly random ingredients, something that might come in handy in their early adult years. And they did. I saw teams contemplating how certain flavors would work together and how to add different textures to their dishes. These weren't things I talked about beforehand. I just gave them the rules, told them they had to create two dishes, directed them to the ingredients and let them go.

HOUSE SPECIALS

Of course, most libraries I spoke with while researching this book soon discovered that offering one food program just wasn't enough. Patrons were clamoring for more. They enjoyed the exposure to ingredients, equipment, and tastes beyond those with which they were already familiar. They found that libraries could be the ideal place for learning about food and community food needs. This section will feature programs and services that are large in scope, requiring more resources but also providing larger or more extensive outcomes.

Cookbook Clubs: Three Variations

One of the most common large-scale programs libraries tend to offer has been book clubs that run from month to month from year to year. These require a large commitment on the part of the library and the patrons to keep the program running and the discussions engaging over time. The three examples highlighted next each demonstrate a different approach to using cookbooks and food as a basis for a monthly club. One of the powers of the cookbook club is its ability to draw in new faces and connect them to the library in ways they hadn't previously imagined.

📖 COOKBOOK CLUB AT STORRS LIBRARY

The cookbook club at the Richard Salter Storrs Library in Longmeadow, Massachusetts, pays homage to community gatherings of old by hosting potlucks inspired by the cookbook of the month. Discussions occur around a community table where members can eat, drink, share, and laugh together.

By Wendy Pearson

After having discovered an article about a cookbook club at a library in California, we decided to host our own and see how well it would be received. Though not initially sure if there would be a need for the program or interest in it, we knew that our cookbook collection circulated well and that our holds shelf often filled up with the latest cookbooks. Plus, we love to cook and eat, so we thought it was worth a try!

Here's how it works: I select a cookbook that has more than thirty available copies in our library consortium of roughly 150 member libraries and place holds for our own library. We keep the books on our holds shelf and patrons pick them up and check them out to their own accounts. Each member selects a recipe and e-mails or calls in their choice in order to avoid duplication. Members, including the library staff members who will attend the program, prepare a dish at home and bring it to the library with serving utensils. The library provides water and coffee, plates, utensils, cups, and napkins.

After a brief introduction, the group serves themselves all the dishes buffet/potluck style. While we are eating, we take turns discussing the recipe we prepared, and the book in general. The book discussions can get quite lively, as many have opinions about the book, its author, and the recipes. We have on hand flyers for next month and copies of the next month's book for patrons to check out as they leave.

We began a lunchtime cookbook club in January 2016 with Ina Garten's *Make It Ahead*. We had twenty-five in attendance for our first session, an impressive number for a daytime program in our small, suburban town of roughly sixteen thousand. Within eight months, we had hit capacity for our program room with thirty-one attendees and had to create a wait list for the program.

Due to the overwhelming popularity, and the cookbook club devotees spreading the word to their working friends, we started an evening session in April 2017 to accommodate the extra people and for patrons whose schedules didn't allow them to attend library programs during the day. Our first evening session had thirteen people in attendance and has hovered around this number, whereas the lunchtime group remains in the twenty-five to thirty range.

Now it's January 2019, and both cookbook clubs remain popular. We even have patrons of other libraries as loyal attendees, having heard through the grapevine about the success of our group. A few months ago, a small group of developmentally disabled teenagers began attending the group with two of their caregivers. Together they prepare a recipe, bring it along, and discuss it with the group. Community in action, food literacy in a fun format, increased circulation numbers, and new patrons walking through our doors. A great idea and a penchant for snacks helped to create a super successful program at Storrs Library.

📖 COOKING THE BOOKS

At the West Boca Branch of the Palm Beach County Library System in Boca Raton, Florida, it's about more than just the food. Cooking the Books members talk about the stories and the places featured in the selected cookbooks. Working around a "no-food" policy, program leaders brought in guest chefs for demos and lively discussions.

By Stacy Alesi

I started Cooking the Books in October 2012 when I noticed that cookbooks were no longer just collections of recipes; there were stories being told along with the food. I loved reading those stories, and I thought if I enjoyed them, maybe other people would as well. I approached my supervisor about starting a cookbook discussion group and his reaction was based on a long-running joke in this area (a highly affluent suburb): What do women in Boca Raton make for dinner on Friday night? Reservations.

Nonetheless, I persuaded him to let me try it for a few months. We have to turn our publicity in for events three months in advance, so I needed to schedule at least three months' worth of cookbook discussions just to get publicity for them. He acquiesced, and to be honest, we were both pleasantly surprised by the turnout.

It had been my experience in this library that getting three to four people for a new program was fine and that it takes time to build up a regular audience. That first month we had a dozen people, mostly women but a couple of men as well. Turned out that one of the men was there to pick up women! He did not return, but the other gentleman did, a recent widower who was learning to fend for himself in the kitchen. Over the years, attendance has varied from about six (during the summer, we have a seasonal population that dramatically increases from October to April) to twenty-five or so. There is a core group of about eight regulars in summer, a dozen in winter, plus "snowbirds," seasonal visitors who go back and forth between home (usually New York, New Jersey, Connecticut, Massachusetts) and Boca Raton. Plus, we always have new people wandering through just to see what's going on. They tend to come and go, and we encourage that.

Over the years, we have done a lot of new cookbooks—I received permission fairly early on to order multiple copies of leased books so we could all read the same cookbook, and other times, we've done themes like Italian food, Latin food, Asian food, vegetarian, pies, holiday cooking, and so on; other themes like cast iron cooking, sheet pan cookbooks, and so forth; plus a favorite that we've repeated a few times, Food Network Stars. We've also done restaurant cookbooks, some of which I was the only one who cooked anything from them like *The French Laundry*

Cookbook by Thomas Keller and *A New Napa Cuisine* by Christopher Koslow. But everyone loved the gorgeous pictures and the stories.

Favorite cookbooks have been *Dining In* by Alison Roman, *The Food Lab* by J. Kenji Lopez-Alt, *The Smitten Kitchen Cookbook* by Deb Perelman, anything by Ina Garten (we've done a few over the years), and *Cravings* by Chrissy Teigen (the best/funniest stories). We recently did *Deep Run Roots: Stories and Recipes from My Corner of the South* by Vivian Howard, and I showed the episode where she went on a book tour (she had a PBS cooking show). The members loved the stories in the cookbook and the TV show, but not the recipes. Interesting, no?

My library has policies against cooking and bringing in food to share, although I have received permission a few times to bring in professional chefs to do demonstrations. We have also done a couple of fiction titles, including *Kitchens of the Great Midwest* by J. Ryan Stradal and *Delicious* by Ruth Reichl. Once a year, usually over the summer, we do a chef memoir, such as *Blood, Bones & Butter* by Gabrielle Hamilton, *Kitchen Confidential* by Anthony Bourdain, *Yes, Chef* by Marcus Samuelsson, *32 Yolks* by Eric Ripert, and so on. We've also done some great courses from the Everyday Gourmet series and one on wine, again usually over the summer, and those have been very popular.

I subscribe to several foodie newsletters—*Eater*, *Taste*, and so on—and always read the new cookbook reviews and see which ones are winning awards. I also read all those best new cookbooks lists that proliferate the Internet. I select all the cookbooks we do, but I'm always happy to take suggestions from members. Some are vegetarian and some only cook organic and we try to accommodate everyone when possible.

I facilitate the discussions and I generally start by asking for a show of hands as to who liked the cookbook and who actually cooked from it. I even have a few regulars who love reading cookbooks but don't generally cook. Some like to copy recipes and share them with their children (most are retirees) and only a few like to bake, so I tend to avoid baking books as a rule. That's been interesting to me, as I love to cook and to bake, but apparently, I'm a bit of an anomaly. When I've done the baking books (only a few over all these years), my regulars tend to grumble, but I invariably get new folks who only come because they like to bake.

We discuss whatever we've made, if the recipe worked as written, or if there are better recipes for the same thing elsewhere. We discuss the stories and the author's voice, and I often show snippets of Google talks or YouTube interviews with the chefs. When we've done restaurant cookbooks, occasionally I get to go to the restaurant and report back—or I ask my son to, he lives in Brooklyn and has gone to Four and Twenty Blackbirds (a pie shop and cookbook) and Ample Hills Creamery (ice cream shop and cookbook) for me. I've been to Gramercy Tavern, Prune (Gabrielle Hamilton), Ink (Michael Voltaggio's restaurant; we did the Top Chef cookbook, and he was a winner) and several others in New York and California.

My favorite story: I went to Scarpetta in Miami and had a fabulous dinner there, including Scott Conant's signature dish, spaghetti with tomato basil. I got an advanced copy of the Scarpetta cookbook and made that recipe. I've made enough pasta to immediately realize that there was something wrong with the pasta part of the recipe, the ratio of flour to liquid was way off. I made the recipe as written and it was a nightmare. I wrote his editor, and they forwarded my e-mail to Conant who had his kitchen test it. Turns out I was right—the recipe was converted from restaurant quantity to home cook quantity incorrectly. They said they would fix it if it went to a second printing. They also invited me to visit the Miami restaurant and said I'd be "taken care of." Whatever that meant. I went with my husband and another couple and was greeted warmly and given a card thanking me for coming. The meal was so-so, the place was packed, the service iffy at best, and the sommelier was only good for recommending the most expensive wines on the list. That card was all they gave me; they didn't offer a drink or dessert or anything, so not sure what they meant by "taken care of!" But my cookbook group loved that story.

RECIPE CLUB

In an attempt to build more social infrastructure in an increasingly high-cost community, the Warren Township Branch of the Somerset County Library System of Warren, New Jersey, turned to food. Rather than focus on a select book, this club builds its gatherings around themes and cooking styles.

By Catherine DeBerry

Due to the cost of living in the state of New Jersey, we started to notice a few trends that were affecting our patrons' quality of life. Residents were slowly moving out of the state due to the high cost of living, resulting in many families living far apart. For those families who continue to live in New Jersey, often both parents have to work. As families lived farther and farther apart and adults spent longer days at work, librarians at Somerset County Library System of New Jersey's (SCLSNJ) Warren Township branch began to notice that their patrons were looking for new ways to engage, to meet new people and to create a larger sense of community.

We realized that one of the best ways to create that sense of community was to re-create the days in which recipes were passed down from generation to generation and were swapped at the church potluck, the bus stop, large family gatherings, and the neighborhood block party. In response, Diane Hahn and I started the monthly recipe club in September 2016. Members of the community gathered monthly and still continue to meet monthly to discuss cooking tips, share family recipes, sample homemade food, and talk about family traditions.

In preparation for the club, we typically decided on topics/themes for the monthly recipe club meetings six months in advance. We would then determine whether it would be staff-led or if we would hire an outside presenter for free. We would typically hire an outside presenter if a certain level of expertise that neither I nor my colleague had was needed for the theme. To prepare for staff-led meetings, my colleague and I would do some background research on the topic, which we would share with the group during the monthly meeting. We would alternate months in which we offered staff-led sessions as they required a great deal of background preparation and research.

Meetings/programs were designed so that all attendees could contribute if they wished to not only encourage socialization but also build a sense of community. We intentionally kept the size of the program to no more than twenty to twenty-five people so that every attendee would get a chance if he or she wanted to share their advice, tips, recipes, and traditions and socialize.

Once we had a core group of attendees, Diane and I also provided or planned for a higher level of patron participation to provide a variety of experiences as well as to offer opportunities for patrons to learn and/or further develop culinary skills. However, regardless of who led the meeting, the patrons who attended always had the chance to share recipes, tips, and food they prepared at home. The opportunity to share recipes or food was typically optional, with patron recipes available in advance of the actual meeting. To further promote the club and get patrons excited, we displayed cookbooks and made cookbook lists on that month's topic/theme available for patrons to take home.

Here are the programs we have offered thus far:

- Everything Italian
- The Momofuku Challenge** *(All participants borrowed the Momofuku cookbook and chose a recipe to make and bring.)*
- Decorating with Fondant, with local baker*, ** *(Patrons made fondant from scratch and learned how to use it to decorate cupcakes.)*
- Growing and Using Herbs for Cooking, with a 4-H community educator*, ** *(Patrons practiced preserving herbs for culinary practices.)*
- Making Candy
- Preserving Jams and Jellies*
- Cookbook Swap** *(Patrons brought in cookbooks they wanted to swap. We included cookbooks that were deselected from the library's collection as part of the swap.)*
- Healthy Eating, with a local grocery store dietician*
- Lighten It Up (Healthier Cooking and Baking)
- Get Ready for Cold Weather: Soups and Stews
- Thanksgiving Day the Easy Way

- Holiday Cooking Traditions and Recipes
- Everything Apples
- Summer Salads
- Digitize/Preserve Your Family Recipes** *(All participants brought in their family recipes and digitized them with the help of SCLSNJ's digitization team)*
- Breakfast All Day
- Fall Harvest Bounty
- Too Hot to Cook
- The Best of Barbeque
- My Favorite Holiday Cookie
- Keepers, the Dinner Plan, and More with Caroline Campion (local food author)*
- How to Host a Tea Party* *(This was led by a patron who served a traditional Persian tea.)*
- Favorite Celebrity Chefs
- Cooking for Two
- Holiday Cookie Exchange ** *(All participants brought cookies to share and exchange.)*

The programs with an asterisk (*) next to them were presented by outside presenters. The programs with two asterisks required more involvement from the patrons either with a hands-on activity, food preparation at home, or more involvement/interaction with each other.

Attendance varied depending on the topic, but on average, it was currently about ten to twelve. At times, the attendance was as large as twenty to twenty-five, particularly when we first started the club. Nearly two hundred recipes have been shared/swapped since the series inception. Today, a core group of fifteen individuals regularly attend the monthly recipe club meetings.

In the process of developing this series, we discovered that one of the features that was most important to the success of the club was to have a moderator / presenter / staff person who is very outgoing and willing to engage and share stories and recipes. While much food was prepared and sampled and garden bounties shared, no one became culinary experts. However, the most important goal of creating a sense of community is where this series of programs has been most successful. Regular attendees know each other by name. Family and cultural traditions and stories are regularly shared. Several friendships were made during these monthly meetings and continue outside the library. And the success of this kind of programming in the SCLSNJ library system has resulted in the development of more programming, which provides for greater patron participation and the development of programming that encourages community engagement.

ON THE TABLE EXHIBITION

Local history is always a big hit in libraries. Combine that with food and a city-wide, yearlong initiative and you're bound to build momentum and make lasting impressions. At the Providence Public Library in Rhode Island, the state released its first food plan in 2017. In response, the library and historical society quickly joined forces to create joint programming and displays that built upon a central food-related theme.

By Karisa Tashjian

Rhode Island is known for our vibrant and entrepreneurial food culture and community. Building on the widespread love of the Rhode Island culinary tradition, Providence Public Library (PPL), along with a network of organizations in Rhode Island, partnered for yearlong programming titled A la Rhody. It so happened that both PPL and the Rhode Island Historical Society both had "food" as their annual exhibition and programming themes for 2017. In addition, Rhode Island's first statewide food plan was released in 2017. We found this theme to be an excellent way to weave together history, culture, and community and highlight local ethnic traditions, locally grown and produced foods, and food insecurity issues.

PPL's exhibition and programming was titled On the Table. We prepared for the program by elevating and contextualizing many of our ongoing programs around the On the Table theme and also used the opportunity to strengthen current partnerships and establish new ones through shared programming. PPL hosted a public launch party complete with a local artist offering an interactive performance using a drone inside the library and homemade Twinkies!

PPL's On the Table educational programs offered "foodies" and "nonfoodies" alike many opportunities to nourish both mind and body such as the Families Cooking Together series, a Meet Your Maker event with the incubator Hope and Main's local food producers, a Snackademics series of author talks and art projects, Food for Thought pursuits such as University of Rhode Island Master Gardening classes and PPL Teen Squad culinary training programs.

The six-month exhibition focused on how a meal at a table anchors us to our daily lives. The exhibition examined changes in American foodways and dining culture through the lens of setting the table. A creative fellow, Keri King, used PPL's collections to create a variety of art around the theme and an extensive exhibition catalog was developed that included the items borrowed from various institutions. Related displays included World War I and II propaganda posters addressing food shortages and rationing, Rhode Island immigrant-created food stories, and the Rhode Island Food Bank Kids Cafés.

CHAPTER 7: HOUSE SPECIALS | **69**

> ## ESSENTIAL COLLECTIONS
> ### Literary Feasts
>
> Books and food have a long and intertwined history. This selection of titles highlights some of the famous literary dishes.
>
> - *Literary Feast: Recipes Inspired by Novels, Poems and Plays.* Barclay, Jennifer.
> - *Fictitious Dishes: An Album of Literature's Most Memorable Meals.* Fried, Dinah.
> - *The Book Club Cookbook, Revised Edition: Recipes and Food for Thought from Your Book Club's Favorites Books and Authors.* Gelman, Judy, and Krupp, Vicki.
> - *Books That Cook: The Making of a Literary Meal.* Goldthwaite, Melissa.
> - *Scone with the Wind: Cakes and Bakes with a Literary Twist.* Sponge, Miss Victoria.
> - *A Literary Tea Party: Blends and Treats for Alice, Bilbo, Dorothy, Jo, and Book Lovers Everywhere.* Walsh, Alison.
> - *The Book Lover's Cookbook: Recipes Inspired by Celebrated Works of Literature, and the Passages That Feature Them.* Wenger, Shaunda.

By working together on A la Rhody, we wanted to maximize the exposure and impact of our programming. We created shared marketing materials and a media campaign that had significant exposure. A la Rhody was a new way of working together for the participating organizations, and we had to establish shared goals, communication channels, and expectations. For PPL, the outcomes of the program demonstrated how we could do library-wide programming—and the resources required to do it at a large scale. PPL's Seed Catalog was also established as part of this effort. Visit the online exhibition here: www.provlib.org/programs-exhibitions/exhibitions/on-the-table.

TEEN COOKING CLASSES

The Stilwell Public Library in Oklahoma is a small rural library located in the heart of the country. They serve a large population of Native Americans living in the nearby reservations, many of whom don't have access to healthy foods. Library staff created their cooking classes in an effort to provide a safe and educational activity for the area's teens that would also teach them with a life skill that they could bring back to their families.

By Kathleen Connelly-Brown

Stilwell Public Library is a small (4,000 square feet) rural library in eastern Oklahoma and a branch of the Eastern Oklahoma District Library System. Our operating budget is $178,000, which provides for materials, staff, operations, and programming. We do get additional funding support from the Stilwell Public Library Friends Society. In addition, as is state law in Oklahoma, all food items used in programming or served must be paid for with funds from special revenue—which is an account funded solely by donations and/or grants.

Stilwell is a rural community (population of 4,000) with a near 50/50 population rate of Native Americans (Cherokee Indian) and Caucasians. Stilwell's poverty rate is quite high (37 percent) and thus the Native American population relies on commodity foods to supplement their nutritional needs. Commodity foods are typically staple items such as flour, baking mixes, oil, and pastas as well as some fresh fruits and vegetables, frozen meat, and fruit juice. Canned fruits and vegetables, shelf-stable milk, and cheese are also included with commodity food distributions.

Breakfast and lunch are offered free at school for all public school students due to the high poverty rate. Many of the rest of our population are on SNAP and WIC. Stilwell also has the distinction of having the lowest life expectancy in the nation at 56.3 years as reported in the *Washington Post* (September 2018)! This is due in part to poor access to high-quality health care, a high rate of obesity and diabetes (especially among the Native American population), lack of access to healthy food, poor diet and exercise, high rate of smoking and drug use (meth). Generations of poverty and unhealthy lifestyles have contributed to this social-cultural impact of low life expectancy.

The Stilwell Public Library (as with most public libraries) plans programs that attempt to meet a need in our community. Based on the poor health of our patrons, I felt it was important to offer something that would expose children to healthy food in a fun way. Personally, I tend to choose a cookie over an apple myself, so I felt that I could understand the difficulty many teens have in trying to break through the social and cultural norms that influence their eating habits. It was important to me personally to encourage teens to learn how to use not only new foods but also foods they may have current access to in new ways. It's always said about teen library programs "Feed them and they will come," but I didn't simply want to feed them; I wanted to teach them. Our cooking class was born from this idea.

I began reviewing recipes that had healthy ingredients and were simple to make. We don't have access to an oven in my library, but we did have other small appliances: a blender, microwave, hot plate (single burner as on a stove), and various cooking utensils. Most of these items were provided to the library as part of a

YOUR BAKING CLUB CHECKLIST

If you are investing in supplies to start a baking club, these are our recommended must-have basics:

- 3 mixing bowls of different sizes
- 1 set of measuring cups
- 1 set of measuring spoons (teaspoons and tablespoons)
- 1 set of spatulas
- 1 set of knives
- 1 pair of oven mitts
- 1 package each of baking essentials—flour, sugar, salt, pepper, baking powder, baking soda
- 1 package of latex-free gloves for food handling
- 1 set of towels for cleanup

If you are lucky enough to have access to a full-service kitchen (in other words—an oven) in your library or your city's community center where you could take the club as outreach, we also recommend the following supplies:

- 1 set of pots with lids (small, medium, large)
- 1 set of cookie sheets
- 1 cupcake tin
- 1 pizza pan and pizza cutter

It is also helpful to have paper plates, disposable silverware, and napkins so the teens can divvy up their baked goods and enjoy them!

grant awarded to the Friends to use in conjunction with the farmer's market that they sponsor. Once I had several recipes that could be made using these tools, I began putting the word out to our teens that we'd be offering food programs and cooking programs to build their interest.

Our first program was smoothies. I found a recipe online that allowed for numerous variations of a smoothie using a method of adding liquid, fruit, vegetables, and an extra. For example, two parts fruit, one part vegetable, one part liquid, and one dash extra. Supplies offered included peaches, pineapple, strawberries (all frozen), fresh blueberries and raspberries, celery, spinach, kale, almond milk, plain yogurt, apple juice, cinnamon, and vanilla extract. The kids were encouraged to think outside the box and choose things that appealed to them on their own and we'd experiment to see what happened.

We did a lot of talking while prepping the ingredients; we talked about how to clean the fresh items, healthy attributes of each item, how it might react to / flavor the other items, and how our end results would taste. Many kids in attendance had never eaten fresh fruit or vegetables before. None had tasted almond milk before and most claimed they did not like yogurt. *All* participants found a combination they liked, and one boy said he was going to ask his mother to buy kale so he could make smoothies with it at home—he liked kale mixed with pineapple, yogurt, and a dash of vanilla.

Our next program was homemade granola bars. This recipe was also customizable with the base being toasted oats, honey, and a small amount of butter. Add-ins included dried cranberries, peanut butter, chocolate chips, macadamia nuts, peanuts, and sunflower seeds. We used the microwave to warm the honey and butter and pressed the mixture into disposable tin pans. I did have to put the bars in the staff room freezer to set prior to cutting, but they turned out well.

I encouraged the kids to use the "cooling time" to clean up because that is also an important part of cooking! Most of the participants did not know you could make homemade granola bars nor had they tasted dried cranberries before. We had a smaller turnout for this program, so each child made an entire 8″ × 8″ pan full of bars to take home. We had the participants share what they made with each other so each one could take home a variety.

The next program was chicken stir-fry. I was nervous about this program because I wanted the kids to learn how to properly cut the vegetables and the chicken, which would require they use very sharp knives—but they did a great job! We learned about knife cuts (julienne and chop), knife safety, cross contamination, and a new method of cooking—stir-fry! We talked about how this dish was fairly economical as the local grocers often have chicken on sale. Kids who said they hated vegetables gobbled this up and expressed a new appreciation for green and red peppers and carrots!

Our final program was a dinner salad made with spinach and a small amount of bacon. The focus of this program was that the greens would take center stage and be filling—my attempt to teach the kids that a "meal" didn't always have to be a portion of meat and potatoes. Plating the dish was also a big focus with this class because the actual cooking portion was so short (cooking the bacon). They learned the expression "You eat with your eyes first" and had fun learning how to set the table and "present" a meal. Since we had a low turnout (again sadly), we invited some other library staff to eat this creation. This provided an opportunity to act as host for the meal. The kids served drinks and sat at the table family style with their "guests."

As mentioned, the biggest outcome was exposing the teens to ingredients and foods they had never tried before. Many enjoyed the new foods and said they would ask their parents to buy them again. Many had never cooked for themselves and thus gained confidence to begin cooking at home. One girl stated she was now cooking once a week to help relieve the burden on her mother.

All participants reported helping more in the kitchen and taking over additional chores such as coming up with dinner plans, dishwashing and cleaning up, and helping with shopping. Average attendance for each program was six teens/tweens (I opened it up to middle school kids as we went along). Because attendance dwindled toward the end of the program run (January through May) and because we were about to switch gears to summer reading programming, the cooking class program kind of died out organically. I have plans to begin again this summer with the hopes of attracting new participants and carrying it through the fall.

Financially, this was a difficult program series to maintain. Part of that is because I overbought ingredients hoping for a larger turnout when I should have bought for fewer participants. The program is best styled as servings enough for one meal (as I did with the stir-fry class) and participants then are given sample portions versus larger individual portions. This would also cut down on waste if a smaller group attends. It took me a couple programs to realize that *each* kid did not have to have his or her own full plate to be successful!

As mentioned previously, food items must be paid from the special revenue account, so I was also concerned about running out of money to continue the program in the long term. There are grants available that would help cover the cost of the program, and I will pursue those soon when I reboot it for summer. It was simply not cost effective to spend $80 on a single program.

We had no major accidents or injuries even when using sharp knives, the hot plate, or cleaning the blender. Safety in the kitchen was emphasized in each class, along with food handling, proper technique, and clean up. I often stressed to the participants that if they cook at home, their parents will appreciate the full process—from planning and shopping to clean up.

My goal in all of this was twofold—get more teens into programs and provide information about healthier eating. While both of those goals were met, I also appreciated the opportunity to teach them so much more. During all programs, we did a lot of talking. We discussed fractions during the smoothie program for example! I asked them what sorts of foods they wanted to learn to cook, and they had great ideas. We discussed where to find recipes and how to review grocery ads to find the best deals. I added many cookbooks for teens to our physical collection and had them on display during class. They also picked up skills that will serve them well in the future as they become more independent.

TEEN BACON CLUB

Bacon. One word with so much savory-ness packed densely within. What began as a carrot to lure in the teens became a popular program series that evolved over time to meet the changing interests and needs of the La Vista Public Library's teen community in La Vista, Nebraska.

By Lindsey Tomsu

My personal philosophy when working with teens is that no idea is too big or too crazy. When I was the teen librarian at the La Vista Public Library in La Vista, Nebraska, one of our long-running programs was our bacon club. This program came about because I told my teens that I would try to make any of their program ideas a reality. In 2011, members of the teen advisory board (TAB) were in love with all things bacon. The idea of having a monthly program devoted to bacon was their crazy idea.

With a fully functional kitchen in our library's meeting room, I was able to make this program a reality that ran successfully for about five years. During each meeting of the bacon club, the teens would basically eat bacon comparing different brands (name brand versus store brand) and different cooking methods (microwave versus oven). Sometimes we'd also make bacon-related crafts (bacon-shaped window clings) and try crazy bacon-flavored things (lollipops, soda). For many years, adults would hear about the Teen Bacon Club and get confused. They would inevitably ask, "You mean baking?" We'd reply, "No, bacon. B-A-C-O-N." In amazement, they'd tell us they wanted to come too!

During the beginning of the 2015–16 school year, the members of the TAB were deciding on what our "core" school year programs would be. When we got to bacon club, a number of the older members who'd be around from the beginning and were getting closer to graduation expressed interest in morphing the bacon club into an actual *baking* club. Many of them expressed fear that they would go off to college and live in a dorm and starve to death because they had no idea how to cook anything. As one of the teens said, "I swear to you—I burn water! How can I survive if I can't even boil water?" Thus the Teen Baking Club was born. The new baking club also coincided with our new adulting 101 program, the POTATO Club (**P**ractical **O**rientation **t**o **A**dulting for **To**morrow), which allowed me to try educating teens on the basic cooking skills they'd need to "survive" as an adult.

We decided to spend some of our leftover summer funds on the necessities we needed for the new club. During the school year, we met once a month, except for March and December when, during spring break and the holiday break, we would have an all-day (11:00 a.m. to 8:00 p.m.) meeting. During the monthly meetings, the teens would have about two hours to experiment with various recipes, but during the all-day meetings, they got to really go *Top Chef* and try more complex recipes that might require a longer amount of time to make. For example, during a regular monthly meeting, we baked cookies, but during an all-day holiday meeting, we made nearly ten recipes—everything from ramen pizza to homemade chili to our own flavored crackers. The overall idea was to provide a fun-based program (the joy of cooking) while subtly inserting the knowledge they would need to cook safely in a kitchen once they were out on their own.

To begin the baking club, we needed basic ingredients and kitchen supplies. At my library, we luckily did not have to pay for food out of the teen programming budget (there was a separate library budget for food items). We knew we were going to have to invest in the actual equipment. However, the great thing about such supplies is that most are reusable after the initial investment! When we purchased the following supplies, it only cost around $30. Plus, for the budget conscious, you don't have to invest in the fancy expensive kitchen equipment—a set of 88-cent teaspoons is just fine! We purchased most of our kitchen supplies at Walmart or our local Dollar Tree. The most expensive item we bought was a pair of silicon oven mitts.

What do you do if you want to offer a baking club but you don't have a full-service kitchen in your library? Luckily, there are a number of options still available! Teens can make a variety of tasty recipes with nothing but a microwave or small appliances that can be borrowed from fellow staff members or the teens' families themselves! We have borrowed Crock-Pots, waffle irons, mini hot plates, electric kettles (which can be used to boil water), and so on. Of course, if you borrow equipment this is a great opportunity to teach teens about sanitary kitchens as I require them to return the items cleaner than we received them! I have often found too that parents are willing to lend us some ingredients that we do not need much of (such as a teaspoon of something for a recipe), which saves money in the long run.

The primary outcome should be that teens have fun and learn to enjoy cooking! The great thing about doing culinary literacy in the library is that most libraries are full of cookbooks teens can pull off the shelves for inspiration! Don't limit yourself to just adult cookbooks. There are some great children's and teen cookbooks too that offer a wide variety of recipes to choose from. Usually, during a TAB meeting, I would have time for the teens to go pull cookbooks from the shelves and look through them for inspiration for the next upcoming baking club meeting. I'd have the teens mark the recipe pages with scrap paper and then I'd photocopy the instructions. After the meeting, I would look over what they picked out, read the step-by-step instructions to make sure the recipe was actually doable (didn't require some weird gadget, didn't take three hours when we only had two hours, etc.) and if it was, budget for the recipe to make sure it wouldn't cost too much to make.

One of my teens' favorite recipes that requires an oven is one for making their own flavored crackers. All one needs is some cheddar Goldfish crackers or plain oyster crackers and a mix of dry seasonings (herbs, sauce mix, etc.). Basically, anything that can be shaken out onto the crackers works! Mix it all in a large mixing bowl and add some vegetable oil to get the seasoning to stick to the crackers. Spread out on a cookie sheet and bake at 350 degrees for ten minutes. This is a great recipe for creativity in the kitchen. We made taco-flavored crackers that were to die for and also, for the fun of it, a crazy concoction that basically had a little bit of everything we had on hand in it (parmesan cheese, honey, rosemary, garlic powder, chili mix, just to name a few). It actually wasn't that horrible of a creation! Being able to freestyle experiment like this was a great chance for them to take charge in the kitchen and also (possibly) learn that it is OK for a recipe to go horribly wrong (without wasting a ton of expensive ingredients)!

One of my teens' favorite recipes that does not require an oven is pizza waffles! All you need is a waffle iron, frozen pizza dough, and pizza toppings. Roll out the dough, cut into waffle squares, place one piece of dough as the bottom, insert your favorite toppings (pepperoni, cheese, etc.), place a top piece of dough, and then cook until golden brown. Dip into some marinara sauce—pizza waffle! These are fun to make and really delicious.

The second outcome is that teens are educated about basic cooking skills while having fun. Everyone knows the joy of making something that you then get to eat. I make sure that each meeting of the baking club covers basic kitchen safety. If someone is sick or not feeling well, they are not allowed in the kitchen (we had a bypass area so they could hang out on that side and still talk to and see what everyone was doing). We also cover basic kitchen hygiene, such as washing our hands before preparation and during preparation (if using different ingredients), along with wearing gloves to prevent germs.

We also discuss safety with kitchen knives and working with the oven or hot burners (e.g., only the person putting/removing things from the oven is allowed to be by the oven when it is open). Many of the teens know their own limits and will not participate in chopping tasks or operating the oven if they do not feel comfortable doing so. And we discuss the importance of food allergies. Many of the teens know what they are or are not allergic to. We do not do anything with nuts in the kitchen. When it comes to other potential foods, we'd always make sure we had multiple options available (so if we make cupcakes, we'd make sure we had chocolate and vanilla options).

Another aspect of culinary literacy they learn is how to read recipes. Sometimes we would have to learn how to convert something if we didn't have the proper tools or we'd need to learn how to double something if we were making a bigger batch. The ultimate benefit is that the teens learn how to create something out of nothing.

And sometimes recipes make more than the teens can eat during the meeting! Bring in fellow staff members and have them try out the goodies or have plates and Saran wrap for teens to take leftovers home for their parents to try. The teens are just thrilled to have "outsiders" try their food and comment on how it tastes. One time, we made fortune cookies that looked horrible, but everyone who tried one actually said they were delicious!

The expected outcomes for a baking club include having the teens learn basic cooking safety practices, basic cooking skills (what the tools are, how to read recipes, how to do measurements, etc.), and the comfort and confidence to work in the kitchen. While they may not be able to cook Thanksgiving dinner on their own yet, they should be able to know how to make spaghetti or bake simple cookies.

What they decide to learn how to bake is up to them. If at all possible, let them choose the recipes and teach them how to make what they want. The actual outcomes are less noticeable because we don't live at home with the teens. What we hope is that they gain more confidence in the kitchen and feel slightly more prepared for living on their own when they head to college that we know they aren't just subsisting off of fast food and ramen!

MOBILE KITCHEN

No kitchen, no problem. At the Pikes Peak Library District in Colorado Springs, Colorado, library staff have responded to the demand for food programs by creating a mobile kitchen kit that can be carted off to whatever location has need of it. With more than two thousand square miles of service area in El Paso County, this mobile kitchen is equipped to serve all fourteen district libraries as well as being available for off-site outreaches.

By Melissa Schloesser

The purpose of the mobile kitchen was to promote healthy living and culinary literacy and to meet the demand of requested classes by patrons/expand and provide more tools to staff teaching culinary classes.

PPLD staff members had already been teaching cooking/food/culinary classes before the mobile kitchen was created. However, in order to teach some of the classes or facilitate some of the culinary programs staff had to find random culinary tools and equipment to make the class/program work. One such program that took place was a teen cooking competition that myself and a teen specialist facilitated. There were four teens competing against each other in the cooking challenge. We set up four cooking stations for the teens to use that included flat griddles, knives, blenders, and various cooking utensils. All of these items were brought in by various staff members to make this program work.

Early 2016, one of our branch managers, Abby Simpson, worked on and received a Healthy Living grant for the Pikes Peak Library District. It was her intent to use some of the grant money to purchase culinary tools to help facilitate healthy cooking classes throughout the district. Abby knew of my culinary education background and that I had taught many healthy living/culinary classes for PPLD in the past, so she approached me and the director of creative services to work on this project.

In the beginning, I just came up with a wish/price list of all the culinary tools that I thought would be good for teaching a wide variety of culinary classes. Abby

ESSENTIAL COLLECTIONS
Fandom

Food and binge-watching go together, right? Let's get off the couch with these tantalizing fandom cookbooks. This list could easily spawn its very own cookbook club.

- *The Unofficial Downton Abbey Cookbook, Revised Edition: From Lady Mary's Crab Canapes to Daisy's Mouse Au Chocolat—More than 150 Recipes from Upstairs and Downstairs.* Baines, Emily.
- *The Wizard's Cookbook: Magical Recipes Inspired by Harry Potter, Merlin, The Wizard of Oz, and More.* Beaupommier, Aurelia.
- *The Unofficial Harry Potter Cookbook: From Cauldron Cakes to Knickerbocker Glory—More than 150 Magical Recipes for Wizards and Nonwizards Alike.* Bucholz, Dinah.
- *Outlander Kitchen: The Official Outlander Companion Cookbook.* Carle-Sanders, Theresa.
- *Wookie Cookies: A Star Wars Cookbook.* Davis, Robin.
- *Doctor Who: The Official Cookbook: 40 Wibbly-Wobbly Timey-Wimey Recipes.* Farrow, Joanna.
- *Fifty Shades of Chicken: A Parody in a Cookbook.* Fowler, F. L.
- *The Official Narnia Cookbook: Food from the Chronicles of Narnia by C. S. Lewis.* Gresham, Douglas.
- *The Geek's Cookbook: Easy Recipes Inspired by Pokémon, Harry Potter, Star Wars, and More!* Lecomte, Liguori.
- *A Feast of Ice and Fire: The Official Game of Thrones Companion Cookbook.* Monroe-Cassel, Chelsea.
- *World of Warcraft: The Official Cookbook.* Monroe-Cassel, Chelsea.
- *An Unexpected Cookbook: The Unofficial Book of Hobbit Cookery.* Oseland, Chris-Rachel.
- *Star Trek Cookbook.* Phillips, Ethan.
- *The Geeky Chef Cookbook.* Reeder, Cassandra.
- *The Geeky Chef Drinks: Unofficial Cocktail Recipes from Game of Thrones, Legend of Zelda, Star Trek, and More.* Reeder, Cassandra.
- *The Unofficial Recipes of the Hunger Games: 187 Recipes Inspired by the Hunger Games, Catching Fire, and Mockingjay.* Rockridge University Press.
- *The Snacking Dead: A Parody in a Cookbook.* Walker, D. B.
- *The Walking Dead: The Official Cookbook and Survival Guide.* Wilson, Lauren.

then had to get approval that this all could be purchased with the Healthy Living grant money. Once established that this project could move forward with the Healthy Living grant money, I thought that having this be a "kit" similar to the other makerspace kits that traveled around the library district would be a good idea. I began researching culinary literacy in libraries and if other libraries were doing something similar to what PPLD was trying to create. I reached out to the few libraries that were also beginning to add or had already added some type of culinary literacy kitchen or space to their library for thoughts and advice on this project. As far as I could tell, at the time and still to date, the mobile kitchen at PPLD would be/is the first of its kind for libraries.

One scenario that really helped me establish how I thought that the mobile kitchen should be set up was the cooking competition that I helped put together and facilitate a few years prior. The idea of having cooking stations where patrons could learn and work together really stuck in my mind. I then began figuring out how much it would cost to have one set of everything. From there, I decided that in order to actually teach a class, having at least three stations with two patrons per station, which would allow up to six patrons to be in a class working together, would be best.

I tried to select tools for the mobile kitchen that would be useful, would be found in a typical kitchen, and would provide culinary literacy. This meant that yes; there are three real knife sets in the mobile kitchen, so while using these tools during a class, patrons could learn the proper way to use these tools. I wanted there to be the capability for actual cooking to take place and not just by a microwave; so I included induction burners and large toaster ovens in the mobile kitchen. There are no flashy tools or gadgets for the most part, just (in my opinion) good culinary tools that are generally available in any kitchen. I wanted patrons to walk away from classes and be able to improve the skills they learned in the class on their own and not have to purchase any tools or crazy ingredients in order to do so.

There were many logistics that had to be considered. The wattage that some of these tools required was one issue. We did not want an older library location to use some of the tools in the mobile kitchen and cause a power outage at their location. I worked with facilities to find the right solutions to include in the mobile kitchen to help counter this issue. Another hurdle was figuring out how the mobile kitchen would be distributed throughout the fifteen different physical locations and maintaining a request schedule for the mobile kitchen. Thankfully, I was able to borrow many of the solutions that the makerspace kits used for transporting and keeping track of the mobile kitchen. I worked with our courier to find the best system that would work for transporting the mobile kitchen.

Since there are so many pieces to the mobile kitchen, the kit was broken down into three different parts: "standard" included knives, cutting boards, rolling pins, other cooking utensils, bowls, and so on; "induction" included induction hot plates and induction-ready pans; "toaster oven" included the toaster ovens and various baking pans that went along with it. Later the Vitamix blenders were added. Teen services had a Vitamix that they were using for their food programs and contributed it to the mobile kitchen as well as gave money toward the mobile kitchen to purchase a second Vitamix blender. Later hand mixers and fondant / gum paste tools were added as well. Staff wanting to use the mobile kitchen can choose which parts they want to use based on what their program requires.

The next step was to make sure that this kit would be properly used. I felt that if we are taking the time to create this official service opportunity, we should have procedures to cover liabilities. Also, I felt that food safety and sanitization needed to be addressed, especially since there now was a larger opportunity to handle raw foods and such. To help cover this, I provided resources for staff that wanted to use the kit to train themselves as well as included a flyer that explained the food handling safety procedures. Along with this, we created an official waiver for the mobile kitchen that patrons fill out when attending a cooking class. It was instilled in staff that this mobile kitchen was not a craft kitchen and was in no way to be used for craft programs. We did not want any chance of contamination.

There have since been many wonderful culinary programs facilitated using the mobile kitchen: truffle making, preserves, jams and jellies, macaroons and macarons, healthy smoothies, cake decorating with fondant and gum paste, and healthy after-school snacks, just to name a few. I hope that in the future, programs can be premade to go along with the kit, making it easier for staff members to facilitate a cooking program at their library without being lost or intimidated by what tools are needed to create a culinary program at their location.

EDIBLE EDUCATION GARDEN

Community gardens are an ideal way for libraries to join the fight against food deserts. The Lake Anne Elementary School in Reston, Virginia, understands this concept firsthand. Their school garden began as a school-centric project and soon became a community landmark, impacting the lives of their students and their families.

By Kim Sigle

It started as a once-a-week fifth- and sixth-grade elective class one spring. We had a small courtyard garden at the elementary school, but it was underused. Revitalizing and adding to it had the potential to be an excellent project-based learning unit that would tie in research, math, and science skills. A number of students expressed interest, so we proceeded.

The students involved wanted to help the school community make the connection that healthy food comes from the earth, understand the process of growing food sustainably, and become familiar with fruits and vegetables that grow locally so that they would be more likely to eat these healthy foods at home or in the school cafeteria. They also wanted to support the more than 45 percent of school families that were considered food insecure.

During our first meeting, we tasted a variety of vegetables. The students then came up with a list of need-to-know questions—what did they want to grow, what could they actually grow in our climate, what resources would they need, which plants did well in the similar gardening beds, how would they go about getting seeds to grow, and so on.

Every week, they added to the garden project by project—starting seedlings, building a vertical herb garden from recycled pallets, and so on. They loved using tools and were excited to be outside. As an eco-school, we ended up on a local gardening tour, and our students loved guiding visitors around our organic vegetable garden along with our bird and butterfly gardens. It was exciting to see them really engaged and excited to share their new knowledge.

A major outcome of the project was whole-community engagement. As students began to explore the garden, their excitement flowed to family and staff members. More and more members of the outside community became involved in our garden. A local gardening organization donated tools to us, and a local grocery store provided a grant to purchase seeds, soil, and other supplies. They also sent a nutritionist to provide resources on healthy eating.

Parents began to volunteer in the garden with their students, which evolved into an education and advocacy program that encouraged families to prepare nutritious snacks and meals from locally grown produce at home. Families were inspired to cook together as vegetables grown in the garden, cookbooks, recipes, and measuring cups were distributed during evening events at the school. Family members gathered around tables, comparing favorite ways to prepare eggplants, peppers, carrots, and okra. Students became more interested in finding additional ways to prepare the vegetables from the garden.

We started thinking that our garden had the potential to not only help teach curriculum but also fill needs in our Title 1 community. Students who grow their own vegetables are more likely to eat them and students with a healthy diet perform better academically.

The garden became a little overgrown over the summer because students had limited access to the courtyard, but in the fall we were able to distribute potatoes and lettuce from the garden, along with other locally grown produce donated by the farmers' market, to all the families that came to back-to-school night. Instead of just a handful of students, the whole school was suddenly involved. We passed out recipes and measuring cups and spoons with the vegetables to encourage parents to prepare vegetables with their children, not only as a way to practice math and reading skills but also as a way to encourage them to try new foods. I loved listening to conversations about the best way to use the variety of vegetables that were laid out in the entry hall.

To continue getting students excited about eating locally grown veggies, we worked with the local high school, which has a culinary arts academy. We arranged field trips so the students could see and taste food prepared by the chefs in training. The high school students were able to develop lesson plans around the food they were using in their demonstrations for the 325 third- through sixth-grade students who came to visit them that year. It was a very positive experience for our students and for the older students who were teaching our students.

The enthusiasm spread, and soon other staff members were helping. We decided to expand the garden to a section of the schoolyard that families would be able to access even when school was not in session. The student service-learning club built raised garden beds and began planting, then asked for volunteers to help maintain the space. Anyone who volunteers in the garden is welcome to take produce. It has been wonderful to see students, families, and staff enjoying the fresh produce.

The school's edible garden continues to grow and support more and more community members. It is amazing to see the way that students of all ages, along with community members, work together to plan, plant, prepare, and share the harvest. This program provides leadership opportunities for students and has had a positive impact on the wider community's lifestyle. With hands-on learning, students and community members authentically gain valuable knowledge about sustainably growing food along with a range of curricular subjects, and at the same time, they practice the important real-world skills of communication, collaboration, and problem solving. The school garden has become a neighborhood gathering place.

I am no longer the school librarian, but I live in the community. I'm pleased to see people in the garden when I drive past the school and know that it is still going strong. I know that many in the neighborhood struggle financially, and I love that they have the opportunity to grow vegetables in a sustainable way through the school's garden program.

TEEN MAKER CLUB

Culinary programs are indeed another form of making. By connecting food with literature and adulting, the Eureka Springs Carnegie Public Library in Illinois found a way to deliver solid programming to their community's teens while preparing them for the world around them.

By April Griffith

The culinary programs that the Eureka Springs Carnegie Public Library delivers as part of our teen maker club represent some of the most popular and well-attended recurring events we host for teens. The need for a food program was identified as our weekly teen programs have evolved and library staff adapted our ideas about what was possible in our space and what would engage and sustain the interest of this particular demographic.

Our teen maker club truly began as a book club at the behest of our teen advisory group (TAG). The TAG members voted on a list of books that we then borrowed in sets from the Arkansas State Library for the purposes of the club. Librarians decided that we would prepare a themed snack and activity for each book to be discussed so that newcomers to book club or anyone who hadn't been able to finish the book would still feel welcome and able to participate.

We watched movie adaptations, made crafts, and played games at these meetings and as the year wore on, we discovered that even the most dedicated teens were no longer interested in completing and discussing assigned library book club reading on top of their homework but were instead showing up to socialize while doing the prepared activity. When the time came to submit a new schedule for requested books in October 2016, we consulted with the teens about whether to continue and the motion to reinvent the program as a maker club was unanimous.

Our first teen cooking program coincided with the final meeting of the teen book club in December. The book selection was the *New Policeman* by Kate Thompson, a book that takes place in Ireland, where we planned to make mini Irish soda breads that would also serve as the snack for the program and would be paired with hot tea. We planned and implemented additional cooking programs as we discovered they were a nice way to explore other topics in a fun and engaging way, such as when we made recipes from Sasha Gong's *Cultural Revolution Cookbook* and talked about Chinese history, or when we made mini baked Alaska flambés and discussed the science behind thermal insulators and protein bonding.

One thing we noticed when doing the initial program and those that followed was that the teens were very enthusiastic to prepare food for themselves and proud of their results, but they had not had much practice in a kitchen. Many times we would step in to help them with what we like to refer to now (in a tongue-in-cheek manner) as "pro-tips." These tips are usually things we have picked up over time as we grown-ups have learned to cook for ourselves—such as prerinsing uncooked rice for a less sticky final product or cracking eggs into a separate bowl to more easily remove any pieces of eggshell that might accidentally fall in.

Sometimes these "pro-tips" were as simple as suggesting someone double-check the recipe before adding an ingredient to the mix. We truly identified the need to have more cooking programs for teens when we realized that this was a life skill they would soon be called upon to use as they left their parents' homes in the next few years and would benefit from the opportunity to practice.

Our teen maker club cooking programs are held in our meeting room—a carpeted space roughly 20" × 30" equipped with folding tables and a smaller 10" × 20" room at the rear where there is a bathroom, a small closet for programming supplies, shelving and chair storage, as well as a very basic kitchen that includes a midsized refrigerator, sink and cabinets, but not much in the way of counter space, stove, or cooktop.

Initially, our limited facilities were seen as a barrier to having any sort of cooking programs, but we have learned to improvise, as with our first experiment in baking soda breads, when one of our librarians brought in a toaster oven from home. As we planned and tried out new and different types of cooking programs, it became a habit to figure out what sort of small kitchen appliances would be needed and to send out a general request to our small staff to see if anyone owned and would be willing to lend one of these for use during the program.

Over time, some of these appliances have been donated by community members for use during these programs, such as a blender, a toaster oven, and a hot plate. The library has been able to purchase a few more of these items as well so that kids can work in groups around multiple stations. In a way, it has been beneficial to have a limited kitchen to work with as we imagine that cooking with simple appliances might be a closer approximation of the initial real-world experiences these kids will have in their first independent living situations. In dorm rooms or shared apartments, it is useful to know how to prepare a scrambled egg in a microwave!

To prepare for a cooking program we first identify and print out or photocopy a recipe and read through it to identify any tricky processes or steps where there might be potential hang-ups. We make a shopping list of ingredients to purchase and, as noted previously, any equipment that needs to be borrowed or brought from home.

About an hour before the program, we set up tables in our meeting room where teens will work in small groups. If the program requires a hotplate or a toaster oven we will set one of these up at each table, along with a single copy of the recipe for teens. All other kitchen tools, anything from a whisk to a towel, and the ingredients, we set out on one large table.

Every cooking program kicks off with the instruction to read the recipe from start to finish before picking up any tools; if a teen immediately leaves their group to grab items from the table it's a good indication that they have not read the recipe all the way through, and they are redirected back to their table to complete this important instruction. We like to place the emphasis on the process of cooking rather than the finished dish and on the fact that it takes practice to get good at doing anything. We know that mistakes will happen and like to point out when we make them ourselves to drive home that concept.

I am not sure what we expected from this program as it evolved into what it is today—it is difficult to summarize expectations because we didn't set any real goals for what has emerged more or less organically. There are some observations that have surprised us and some valuable hindsight that is worth mentioning, however.

Our cooking programs have been very popular with boys who come to the library primarily to use the computers and who don't attend many other programs. They seem to enjoy practicing and honing their cooking skills, which is something we didn't anticipate!

We've also found that our library teens are up for more challenging cooking tasks. We discovered a small batch of canning cookbooks and decided to try making and canning lemon curd—a more labor-intensive process that requires extra care be taken to sanitize the jars for food preservation safety. It felt like a risky endeavor to undertake with usually boisterous teens, but as it turned out, the extra care required to complete the project caused participants to really focus on the process and work together to make sure everything came together.

Finally, we have learned that it helps to plan for a good amount of time for cleanup. It should come as no surprise that cooking is a messy process and I suppose that we librarians have learned from our own experiences to be a little more careful when mixing and pouring, but our teens are still practicing, and along the way, they have caused some epic spills! When the program ends and all the teens have vanished, it can be overwhelming to face a mess of this proportion, so we now make sure to emphasize the importance of cleaning as they go, and set the expectation that everyone will help with the washing up after the food has been enjoyed.

COOKING WITH THE KIDS

Yes, kids can cook too. At the Elmont Public Library in Hempstead, New York, library staff redesigned a popular series of food programs that revolved around sweets to focus more on healthy options and healthy cooking.

By Nadine Spano

In the ten years that I have been a children's librarian, food programs have always been the easiest and most successful programs to run. In library terms, "success" is defined by the number of children who attend. A full house for a program is a success. No one can seem to turn down a program called Chocolate Everything. It's easy to book, easy to fill, easy to run. Success, right?

The year before I became the department head for children's services here at the Elmont Library, I was the night and weekend substitute. I watched children and families fight for spots in the offered food literacy programs. I listened to children cry when it was too full for them to join in and saw parents hover outside the door vying for a glimpse of their child decorating a cupcake. It might have been a success on paper, but as a literacy professional, I knew we could do better.

When I became the head of children's services, I analyzed our food programs carefully for a year. Sweets and cupcakes were a win. Healthy cooking? Not so much. Despite the request from some parents for a nutrition-filled cooking class, they brought in significantly fewer children and much less excitement. "This smoothie is warm and green...*blechhh!*" In no time, the spinach and kale smoothie had little to no attendance. It wasn't just food programs experiencing a shift. Other more popular programs such as anything with bubbles, dinosaurs, sharks, paint parties, characters, and so on seemed to cause that same parental chaos at the door. Parents and grandparents, aunties and uncles, older siblings, younger siblings, everyone wanted to peek in on the fun stuff. It was distracting, and it also got me thinking—family.

In a time when family togetherness is few and far between, where everyone has in earbuds and is immersed in their individualized, screen-perfect world, families who come to the library are craving real-world experiences—and not just for their children! Adults are nostalgic for the things they used to do. Many of these grown-ups use technology but didn't grow up as tech natives. They did things with their families—tangible things and things that took patience and time and problem solving, such as our gingerbread house–making program during the holidays. Like the cupcakes, this was one of the most highly anticipated events of the year. I thought it was the spirit of the holidays and the candy, but was it? With more observation, I discovered it was because it was a *family* event. The joy was in the doing. Enter family cooking.

Immediately following our 2017 gingerbread program, I knew we needed to do this regularly. I wanted families participating, working together, making memories, and spending time in their community with their neighbors. What better place than the library to talk and socialize over food and fun? Research shows that families that cook together at home tend to eat healthier too. For preparation, I reached out to one of our favorite food programmers and asked if she'd ever consider a monthly family cooking program. She loved the idea. We decided to alternate a savory with a sweet and incorporate healthy kitchen habits into our program.

We agreed to twenty families per session and scheduled it the last Wednesday of every month running from January to May. I named it Cooking with the Kids. Together with the programmer, we chose themed nights and a menu that was both fun and easy and took a full hour to complete. We started with a January Super Bowl snack time, February Chinese dumplings, March butterfly cakes, April Cinco de Mayo, and May Memorial Day cake.

Twenty families could bring in an excess of sixty people per program. Thankfully we have a big meeting room space, but this also meant preparing our custodial staff for a major cleanup. I also had to decide on some age limits. I have come to learn that although it is fun to have babies and toddlers exposed to new environments, it can also be a hazard to them and to others when not careful. I spoke to my chef who told me that she likes families to be very hands on and will bring sharp cooking implements as well as hot oil. I made the decision to promote this for children ages five and up with an adult. "No children under the age of five will be permitted."

The first night I definitely heard my share of disappointed parents who swore that their toddler would remain in the stroller the entire time. When I explained that there would be bubbling hot oil and knives around the room, they respected the set safety limits. These boundaries weren't a problem going forward.

Our community, like others, has many dietary restrictions, so chef and I decided to offer vegetarian options especially when it came to the Chinese dumplings that are typically pork. Offering the vegetarian and a chicken option was great . . . until we ran out of the nonpork offering. Chef managed to swap out a few and move things around, but going forward, we learned a lot about what to offer our community.

Each month we had a full registration of twenty families and a waiting list. Of course, there were some months, especially in March, where the weather was just awful. But most of the classes were full and if they didn't fill up with those that signed up, we were sure to recruit families in our children's room to join in. No one ever turned down our Cooking with the Kids Night!

For outcomes, I expected this to be a popular program simply based on the fact that it was food. Like other food programs, I knew that it would be a "success." My goal was to create a real-world experience. My mission was to see the joy of families making memories together, learning about food, food preparation, and meeting one another. This program was designed to create shared experiences with family. But beyond that, it created shared experiences for families within the community. Families met their neighbors. Children made friends. Each month families came together, remembered one another, and talked, laughed, shared. It was no longer the "food" that was popular, but the joy in the activity. From a numbers standpoint, my goal was to decrease the cost per person of food literacy programs while increasing the number of people who experienced it. This proved true and beyond my expectations. Comparing 2016 to 2018, our cost per person for our children's food literacy programming went from $12.12 in 2016 down to $8.07 in 2018. In 2016, we held sixteen food programs, whereas in 2018, we held seventeen. At the same time, the participation in these programs increased by 283 people, or 41 percent. Libraries are about giving and sharing, and I call that a success! Overall, family food literacy programs, when positioned as a shared experience, can make a positive impact on programming numbers and on the social/emotional growth of families and help turn neighbors into a community, all the while making a very small impact on the budget. We are continuing our Cooking with the Kids for another year, and we are growing our family programming and family events library-wide.

 EAT PLAY GROW

Eat Play Grow is an LSTA grant-funded program meant to educate on the importance of food in a young child's life. The Elyria Public Library System in Ohio saw this as a good fit for a steadily growing population with many young families.

By Danielle Coward

The Elyria Public Library System (EPLS) serves the 63,650 residents of the Elyria City School District and the Keystone Local School District with five physical branches and a bookmobile. In 2016, library staff learned of a State Library of Ohio grant to allow public libraries to enhance their summer reading programs with activities that support individual and community well-being. One of those activities was the Children's Museum of Manhattan's EatPlayGrow Curriculum.

EatPlayGrow is a free curriculum developed by the Children's Museum of Manhattan along with the National Institutes of Health to promote healthy habits to parents and young children in an engaging manner. The program includes a storytime with fiction and nonfiction books and music, a craft, a playtime focusing on large motor skills, and parent handouts.

At that time, EPLS was involved in multiple collaborations in the community that included a focus on increasing access to physical activity and healthy food options for residents as well as making sure that children were ready to start school. This community involvement revealed that healthy eating habits and activities needed improvement in our service district and that these issues began at a young age. Statistics backed up these concerns. The city of Elyria is an urban area with a population of 54,533, including 3,745 children under the age of five. Twenty-two percent of the residents live in poverty, and the obesity rate for the city is 71 percent. The Keystone Local School District service area is rural, with a total of 11,216 residents, including 565 below the age of five. While the population has a lower poverty rate, 69 percent of the population is obese. For these reasons, the EatPlayGrow curriculum appeared to be a perfect match for EPLS.

EPLS applied for and received the State Library of Ohio's grant, which provided $1,500 of federal funds with a $500 local cash match. EPLS prepared to pilot the eleven-session curriculum at two of our branch locations: the Keystone-LaGrange branch and the West River branch in Elyria. The weekly sessions would begin in May and continue through August. One class would be off-site at a local community college, where a chef would lead parents and children in making a healthy meal. Librarians began to purchase materials for the program as well as to go through and fine-tune the programming for their respective spaces. Materials purchased included books, demonstration models of food, music, arts and crafts supplies, and supplies for physical activities, including balance beams and tunnels.

EPLS promoted the program aggressively. Our PR department included information on EatPlayGrow in our quarterly newsletter, which is sent to twenty-eight thousand homes. We also promoted the program through posters, bookmarks, and social media. Our community partners helped promote the program, and we sent out an additional 1,175 flyers to local preschools.

Prior to the start of the programs, our online registration was filled up for EatPlayGrow at both locations. The plan was that we could accommodate sixteen parents and children at our Keystone location and thirty-two parents and children at our Elyria location. Despite the online registration, we had some people show up without registration and registered participants who did not show up, so we never had to turn anyone away. Storytime attendance was low at our Keystone branch in the spring of 2016; we often only had one or two children per session. During EatPlayGrow, we had ninety-three program attendees at that branch, averaging nine attendees per session (no one from the Keystone group attended our chef-lead class in Elyria). We had 219 attendees at our West River Branch, averaging nearly 20 per session.

For assessment and evaluation purposes, program participants were given an initial and final survey as well as weekly librarian observations of participants' willingness to try new food and comfort with physical activity. Focus groups were also conducted to get input about the program content and presentation as well as to share any thoughts about the effects of the program on their children.

The surveys showed that 80 percent of parent participants felt they were more informed on child health issues after the class, with more parents able to answer corrections correctly about portion size and the five food groups. Over the course of the program, librarians observed that children were usually willing to try even unfamiliar foods when presented with them after the program. Many children were initially hesitant about the activity portion of the programs but became more enthusiastic as time went by. During focus groups, caregivers expressed surprise over how much of the information the kids had really absorbed as well as how willing the children were to try unfamiliar foods. Many of the children were talking about what they had learned at EatPlayGrow at home.

We felt EatPlayGrow was successful beyond our expectations, both in what the parents and children learned and their enthusiasm for the program. So much so that, after taking a year off for our preschooler participants to head off to school, we hosted this program again at our Keystone branch in 2018.

In 2018, we repeated many of the elements of the program that we felt were successful in the 2016 program, including our promotional efforts, our use of EatPlayGrow's descriptions of the program, and of course, the EatPlayGrow curriculum. The success continued, with our tiny branch averaging thirteen patrons a week for a ten-week program. In addition, because we still had the supplies from the 2016 program, we were able to run this program for only a little more than $200, which was spent on food samples and craft supplies. This $200 was provided by one of EPLS's collaborative partners, Keystone Empowers You.

 FOOD ED

I met Morgan at SXSW 2019 in Austin, Texas. She and I were both attending a food track session on the future of food. As another librarian interested in food, we hit it off, and I was thrilled to hear about her library's innovative food business education program, Food ED. Food ED, at the Mid-Continent Public Library in Kansas City, Missouri, is one of the first of its kind that I've seen—a library-coordinated workshop and conference on the business of food.

By Morgan Perry

My favorite pizza in the Kansas City Metro came from a place called The Fuzzy Pig. They used locally sourced, thick smoked bacon, peaches, a mild cheese, and a little pepper. It was magic! Unfortunately, I haven't had a bite of this tasty treat in the last three years because the food truck that served it did not last to their eighteen-month mark.

The owners had retired from corporate America after twenty-five-plus years, emptied their 401k, and spent their savings on an eighteen-month venture that ultimately failed, landing them right back in the workforce. These were smart, capable, professional people. They had a business plan and a pizza oven straight from Sicily. So how did this happen? And more important, what can public libraries do to help?

Food ED, a part of Square One Small Business Services by Mid-Continent Public Library, was designed to address these sorts of challenges in the food industry.

We are extremely lucky in Kansas City that there is a thriving business resource community with a nonprofit to help organize and promote services. All of this is due to the Ewing Marion Kauffman Foundation and their dedication to funding research and support, not only for flashy tech companies but also for the small businesses that make up the backbone of the United States, and Kansas City in particular.

With so many resources available, we were able to specialize our services. This opportunity for specialization allowed us to narrow our focus to better serve underrepresented groups, such as the food industry. Additionally, we heard from the head of the city's business liaison office that there were record numbers of businesses applying for mobile food licenses. Obviously, the need for food-specific services is very real.

Food is the great equalizer. We all eat, and food permeates nearly every aspect of culture. The food industry attracts people who are driven to create for the service of others. In fact, in a survey we sent out to customers who had taken our Food ED courses, the number of people who wrote that they wanted to "serve others" was astounding. Mobile food businesses such as catering, food trucks, and food products are a great opportunity for vulnerable populations, due to their low entry barrier.

These audiences are often the ones who are most attracted to this entrepreneurial opportunity.

One of our first goals was to strike a balance in our services between what we *want* businesses to know, what businesses *ask* to know, and what they will *actually show up for*. Unfortunately, when we began implementing our mission to help entrepreneurs, very few food businesses were asking for help. Even with more than two hundred resource partners doing programming and offering services in the area, we noticed food business owners were not attending entrepreneurial programs.

To prepare for our new program, we did something that's too often uncommon: we asked our target customers what *they* wanted. See, our mission is to change libraries from the information warehouses they've always been into experiential learning centers based on customer interview–driven decisions. We continually ask ourselves if we are focusing on a topic or using a format because it is easier for our organization or if we are doing it because it works for our customers.

We asked food businesses where they were getting their help. The overwhelming response was that they weren't. They didn't identify as a "real business" and when people did try out SCORE classes or take courses at their local community college, they discovered there was an expected level of knowledge about business terms and culture that was embedded into the curriculum.

We also broke down the challenges for our target customer. If you have the money to take a class or work with a coach, you most likely don't need the free opportunities the library provides. This led us to really assess our customer demographics.

Our adult education brand at Square One is taking practitioners that are successful and helping them learn to teach others how they do what they do. This is a huge departure from using professional presenters. When programmers assume the interests or basic skill level of the customer they are presenting to, they usually get the formula wrong and miss their education goal. By working with these people on transferring their knowledge into teachable moments for a classroom setting, we had the added benefit of learning to be better business specialists.

Our overall expectations for the program were high turnout and enthusiastic participation. However, whereas our turnout is high, there is still a disconnect between the library and the actual business owners. When surveyed, 70 percent of respondents reported that they ask their mentor for assistance whenever they need help. Additionally, when asked to rank six different resources, the library ranked last, even behind a paid financial advisor. We discovered that while we facilitated and organized the events, most people failed to associate the library with the resources themselves, even though 84.1 percent of attendees believed they gained valuable knowledge or skills by utilizing the Library. Our primary struggle is in maintaining a connection with these would-be entrepreneurs and helping them maximize their use of available resources. We believed that quality of information would correlate with frequency of use. However, this doesn't necessarily seem to be the case.

Despite this, our Food ED program fills a service hole in our business resource community. We can see this through the survey results:

- 66 percent of participants in the Food Truck Workshop have never worked in a food business
- 64 percent of participants in the Food Truck Workshop have never eaten at a food truck

These participants had signed up for a six-hour workshop and their participation denotes a level of commitment to opening a business, but never having eaten at a food truck or never having worked in a food business is worrisome.

Our program has grown from four programs a year in 2014 to 145 programs a year in 2018. Growth on that scale in a relatively short time only made sense when we used programming to address multiple aspects of the life of an entrepreneur. This chart from the Ewing Marion Kauffman Foundation research team helped inform our choices beyond the topic "how to start a business" and move us into a mind-set of offering programs that support small business owners.

The addition of *convene* and *celebration* elements to our programs helped us build trust with the community and dramatically improved our reach. We also began to see access as not just offering a topic but offering information/topics in multiple formats, different times of year, and unique instruction styles, including our newest addition—peer learning with P2PU, http://p2pu.org.

Gaining context for the business resource community was also critical to provide quality information to our customers. Instead of positioning ourselves to target high-yield, high-growth companies, we choose to market to those not already being served. We focus on basic business needs for labor market information (LMI) businesses, not the information and technology start-up ecosystem. That looks like offering a solid foundation (pre-101 level courses to position LMI businesses for further learning and letting the technology incubators do what they are best at). We first identified the holes in what's currently offered by the business resource community and then leveraged our library's resources to help people that were not being supported by our community partners.

Once we identified the right customer, we could identify the best community partners to align ourselves with for cross promotion and resource sharing. For example, we leveraged our databases to partner with SCORE mentors (www.score.org) who present the research portion of their classes and encourage their mentors to send their mentees to meet one-on-one with our business librarian to complete their business plans. This benefits the SCORE mentors by being able to provide

Table 7.1 **Choices for type of activity**

Purpose (pick two)	Method	Approach
Educate	Competition/pitch	Experiential
Connect	Lecture	Interactive
Do	Discussion	One-on-one
Inform	Speaker / panel	Presentational
Influence	Social event / happy hour	Virtual
Convene	Mentorship	
Celebrate	Internship	
Fund	Hands-on	
Develop	Online	
Collaborate	Hackathon	
Inspire		

their clients with a better mentor experience. The client can make calculated business decisions by utilizing the resources at the library.

No matter the size of your library system, the first step you should take to start a small business program will be the same. Perform potential customer interviews to help you set aside your assumptions and create an experience based on your customers' needs. You must get in there and ask!

One of the main ways a library can provide service to their business customers is through one-on-one sessions with a business specialist. This is one of the core services Square One Small Business provides. It's in a situation like this that our traditional librarian peers often become nervous. We incorrectly assume that anyone who owns a business already knows more than we do by virtue of the fact that they own said business. And yet, whereas our food business owners generally are experts in making a meal, they are rarely experts in the entrepreneurial side of things.

Time and time again, we hear reference librarians say they do not know enough about business to help customers. The secret is that having a one-on-one with a small business owner is the same as any other reference interview. Through dialog, the librarian discovers what the customer needs and points them to the correct resources. The difference comes at the end of the interview: instead of stopping when we have helped a customer find that specific article, book, or database, we then aid them further by introducing them to a class that will help them apply the information.

There will be, of course, a learning curve for reference librarians, but with time and experience, it's easy to learn to translate the customer's needs and direct them to the best resources.

Ultimately, what public libraries can do best for food businesses is serve them just like we serve any reference customers, with only the one additional step. If you have the budget to hire a team, that's great! Make sure they are diverse and bring different perspectives and experiences to the table. Nonlibrarians can be an asset when addressing populations that aren't walking into your branches already. However, if you don't have the budget for a team or extensive programming, you can still have a huge impact on the business community. Remember that they might be experts in their product or service but probably are not experts on business. Utilize the free and well-curated resources online through organizations such as SCORE and the SBA.

My favorite pizza place in the city would probably still be around if a free, reliable resource organization had been there to coach those entrepreneurs and shore up the gaps in their knowledge. The library can be this resource. As we continue forward, we will help as many people as possible go beyond their business plan and utilize the available resources to create a profitable business.

CONCLUSION

Go Forth and Bake It

As demonstrated by the many examples provided in this book, both cited in the early chapters and included as case studies in the later chapters, food literacy can mean many things. It can be as simple as showing a documentary and facilitating a discussion afterward, or as advanced as a series of food business education tracks and workshops. No matter the size of the library or the makeup of the population, everyone eats, and food literacy programs and services can make a difference in those communities.

It is my hope that the information and stories featured in this book not only will serve as a practical guide for implementation but will, more importantly, prod other libraries into action. As the food landscape in our world changes, so too must we change to ensure better lives for our patrons and ourselves. Food is a uniting concept. Let it unite us in implementing change and helping make the world a better place.

APPENDIX A

COLLECTION DEVELOPMENT

Good news! Most libraries are already providing food literacy resources to their communities through their valuable and well-curated collections. This is something we library professionals do really well, and there are already a handful of books and resources to guide the savvy collection manager. When it comes to building or maintaining a culinary collection, here are a select few titles that are targeted to (or have sections targeting) this specific topic:

Stoeger, Melissa Brackney. *Food Lit: A Reader's Guide to Epicurean Nonfiction.* Santa Barbara, CA: Libraries Unlimited, 2013.

Vnuk, Rebecca. *The Weeding Handbook: A Shelf-by-Shelf Guide.* Chicago: ALA Editions, 2015.

Subject Lists

Beyond books, library professionals understand that the best way to eat an elephant is one bite at a time. When building or refreshing a library collection, it's best to break a topic into its component pieces to see what's missing or what we might have too much of. Here follow a few helpful lists that do just that:

Dewey Decimal System Summaries

395	Customs, etiquette, manners
630	Agriculture
633	Field and plantation crops
634	Orchards, fruits, forestry
635	Garden crops, horticulture
636	Animal husbandry

637	Processing dairy and related products
639	Hunting, fishing, and conservation
640	Home and family management
641	Food and drink
642	Meals and table service
663	Beverage technology
664	Food technology

Library of Congress Subject Headings

TX1–1110	Home economics
TX301–339	The house: arrangement, care
TX341–641	Nutrition, foods, and food supply
TX642–840	Cooking
TX851–885	Dining room service
TX901–946.5	Hospitality, hotels, food service
TX950–953	Taverns, barrooms, saloons
TX955–985	Building operation and housekeeping

Business Topics

Libraries have begun to recognize their unique positions within communities as business incubators. Many, like those in the case studies earlier, are actively engaging their local businesses and nonprofits in designing business education opportunities. Here are some areas within the food industry that libraries can look to for inspiration.

Bakeries	Food carts	Private chefs
Bars	Food critics	Restaurants
Breweries	Food developers	Specialty shops
Cafés	Food trucks	Street vendors
Catering services	Food writers	Wine bars
Coffee shops	Franchises	Wineries
Cottage foods	Gastropubs	
Distilleries	Personal chefs	

Cooking Methods

Books that focus on a particular cooking method have always been popular, as many home cooks have a particular favorite method they return to time and again. This list can help guide collection managers in covering their bases.

Dry Methods

Baking	Frying	Sautéing
Barbequing	Grilling	Smoking
Broiling	Panfrying	Solar oven cooking
Deep fat frying	Roasting	Stir-frying

Wet Methods

Basting	Poaching	Steaming
Blanching	Pressure cooking	Stewing
Boiling	Scalding	Tempering
Braising	Simmering	Thermal cooking
Caramelizing	Sous vide	

Other Techniques

Brining	Drying	Pickling
Canning	Fermenting	Seasoning
Creaming	Historic methods	
Dredging	Marinating	

Cuisine Styles

Within bookstores, cookbooks are often arranged via marketing categories, such as the cuisine styles listed next. Cuisine styles can be technique based but are often trend or movement based. This list touches upon some of the more popular styles.

Farm to table	Molecular	Soul food
Fast food	New American	Sous vide
Fusion	Note	Vegan
Haute cuisine	Nouvelle	Vegetarian
Modernist	Slow food	Zero waste

Diets

If libraries know one thing for sure, it's that diet cookbooks are *always* in demand. Diets and dieting trends are also an ever-shifting landscape in the public awareness, with new fad diets coming out nearly every month. Here are the more prominent diets that have been popular in North America for the past few years.

The 4-Hour Body	Alkaline diet	Blood type diet
5:2 diet	Baby food diet	Detox diet

Dukan diet
Fruitarianism
Gluten-free diet
Immune power diet
Israeli Army diet
Juice fasting
KE diet
Macrobiotics
Master cleanse
Paleolithic diet
Pritikin diet
Scarsdale medical diet

South Beach diet
Superfood diet
Weight Watchers, or WW
Low-carbohydrate diets
- Atkins diet
- Salisbury diet
- Stillman diet
- Sugar Busters
- Zone diet
- Ketogenic diet
- Whole30 diet
High-carb / low-fat diets

- Eat More, Weigh Less
- The Good Carbohydrate Revolution
- The Pritikin Principle

Food combining
- Fit for Life
- Suzanne Somers's Somersizing

Liquid diets
- Cambridge diet
- SlimFast

Equipment

Another cookbook trend that has recaptured audiences is the equipment-based book. These cookbooks have long been popular; as new appliances and kitchen accessories have been released over time, cookbooks specializing in their capabilities have been released and quickly snatched up. Crock-Pot cookbooks dominated the 1970s, and now in the 2010s, we have instant pots.

Air Fryer
Bain-marie
Blender
Broiler pan
Cast iron cookware
Casseroles
Charbroiler
Clay pot
Crock-Pot / slow cooker
Deep fryer
Dutch oven

Food processor
Flat-top grill
Griddle
Grill
Instant cooker
Microwave
Mixer
Muffin pan
Oven
Panini grill
Pressure cooker

Range top
Rice cooker
Sheet pan
Smoker
Solar oven
Sous vide cooker
Tagine
Waffle iron
Wok

Nutrition Topics

Nutrition can be just as daunting for the collection manager as it can be for the library patron. This handy checklist of nutrition topics can be used to determine what materials a library already has and what gaps might exist in this area.

Appetite
Additives
Carbohydrates

Cholesterol
Detox
Diet and exercise

Digestion
Disease prevention
Eastern diet

Eating disorders	Food addiction	Raw foods
Eating patterns	Hunger	Sugars
Energy budget	Minerals	Vitamins
Fasting	Pregnancy, babies, and children	Water
Fats		Western diet
Fiber	Proteins	

Popular World Cuisines

It should come as no surprise to any librarian out there that perhaps the most popular types of cookbooks have always been world cuisines. Here is a list of noted world cuisines that have graced our library shelves for decades alongside some of the more recently popular cuisines.

American	Historic cultures	Nigerian
Brazilian	Indian	Pakistani
British	Iranian	Persian
Cajun	Israeli	Peruvian
Cantonese	Italian	Polish
Caribbean	Japanese	Polynesian
Chinese	Korean	Spanish
Creole	Lebanese	Thai
French	Mediterranean	Turkish
German	Mexican	Vietnamese
Greek	Middle Eastern	
Hawaiian	Moroccan	

Types of Food and Drink

Of course, another way to review the makeup of a library's foodie collection is to look at the categories topically—specifically in regard to food groups and types of food.

Alcohol	Condiments	Legumes
Alternative foods	Dairy	Leftovers
Beer	Eggs	Live cultures
Brassicas	Fats and oils	Meat
Breads	Fish	Milk
Cake	Fruit	Mushrooms
Cheese	Grains	Noodles
Chilies	Herbs	Pasta
Coffee	Juice	Pastry

Seafood
Shellfish
Soy
Spices

Spirits
Superfoods
Tea
Vegetables

Wine
Yogurt

Western Meals and Menu Categories

Yet another way to categorize the collection in regard to food and cookbooks is to look at food and meals by occasion. Entertainment has many subcategories, listed here.

Á la carte
Antipasto
Appetizers
Banquet
Breakfast
Brunch
Buffet
Celebrations
Dessert
Dinner
Elevenses
Entertaining

Entrée
Family style
Haute cuisine
Hors d'oeuvre
Linner
Lunch
Main course
Picnic
Pinchos
Plat du jour
Platter
Potluck

Salad
Sandwich
Sides
Snack
Soup
Starter
Supper
Tapas
Tasting
Tea

APPENDIX B

TOOLS FOR THE COMMUNITY FOOD ASSESSMENT

Community Food Assessment: Readiness Questionnaire

	Questions	Considerations	Yes	No
1	Has a community food assessment been done in your region?	Are there adjacent assessments or assessments with overlapping values that you can seek access to?		
2	Is there community interest in your local food system?	Are there clear issues that your community wants to challenge?		
3	Has your organization articulated clear questions it wants to pursue via a community food assessment?	What are your starting objectives? What kinds of programming and resources does your organization provide?		
4	Who are the stakeholders that might be engaged in seeking answers to your questions?	Do they have the time and skills to commit? Would the findings inform other work?		
5	Has your organization identified subject experts to assist with the process?	Do they have the time and skills to commit? What skills might you need?		
6	What resources have been identified for possible use in a food assessment?	Have grants been considered? Are stakeholders able to contribute? Who will lead these efforts?		
7	How will the results of the food assessment be shared?	Would the assessment inform other work in your community? Is local government interested in the results? What formats might you utilize?		

APPENDIX B: TOOLS FOR THE COMMUNITY FOOD ASSESSMENT

Community Food Assessment: Laying the Foundation

Build your team

What will we call ourselves?	

Who are the members of the planning team?				
Name	Organization	Contact information	Resources and skills	Role

How will we operate?				
Roles	Meetings	E-mail	Phone	Other

Brainstorm and discuss the food assessment				
Why are we doing this?	What are your values as an individual?	What are the values team members have in common?	What problems need solving?	What do we need to know?

APPENDIX B: TOOLS FOR THE COMMUNITY FOOD ASSESSMENT

What are our core questions?

1.
2.
3.

How will we define our community?

Where are the boundaries?	How does that community identify itself?	What groups are included?	What do we already know?	What data is already available?

What people or organizations will we ask to help?

Community Food Assessment: Work Plan Template

Phase	Actions	Tools/resources	Responsible	Deadline	Notes
Prework	Assess readiness				
	Research existing data				
	Talk with others who have conducted assessments in your area				
Build a team	Identify key stakeholders				
	Assign roles				
	Develop planning and decision-making process				
	Schedule meetings				
Lay the foundation	Determine core questions				
	Define community				
	Brainstorm other partners				
	Determine available resources (including grants and in-kind donations)				
	Develop time line				
	Create work plan				
	Recruit participants and experts				

Phase	Actions	Tools/ resources	Responsible	Deadline	Notes
Plan and conduct assessment	Plan for meaningful community participation and engagement				
	Develop a communication plan				
	Identify appropriate research methods				
	Design research tools				
	Collect data from existing and original sources				
	Process and analyze data				
Finalize	Summarize findings				
	Present and disseminate findings				
	Evaluate process				
	Celebrate				
	Develop next-steps action plan				

APPENDIX C

INTERACTIVE WEBSITES, TOOL KITS, AND MOOCS

American Culinary Federation. "ACFEF Apprenticeships."
www.acfchefs.org/ACF/Education/Apprenticeship/.
At this site, you can access the database of accredited culinary secondary and post-secondary programs and apprenticeships and understand the accreditation process. The ACF also provides information to scholarships.

Bertlesen, C. "Online Cookbooks and Other Culinary Materials: Sources."
Gherkins and Tomatoes. https://gherkinstomatoes.com/online-cookbooks-sources/.
Cynthia D. Bertelsen is a food blogger, and this particular post is a treasure trove of links to digital cookbook and menu collections across the web. All collections are digitized and include such gems as advertising cookbooks, community cookbooks, historical cookbooks from around the globe, and menu libraries. These links can easily eat up hours of your time. Pun intended.

Chef's Resources: Culinary Knowledge for Professional Chefs and Culinarians.
www.chefs-resources.com.
This site has a wealth of resources for chefs and foodies. Food profiles explain terminology and delineate among various types of foods or food products (i.e., fish cuts and flavor profiles). The "Kitchen Management Tools" section provides worksheets for food cost calculations, inventory balances, and recipe templates. Other offerings on the site include tool and equipment reviews, online classes, job postings, and more.

Community Commons. www.communitycommons.org/home.
Community Commons is an organization devoted to researching and advancing community health. They are best known for their collection of resources for data mapping, webinar offerings, and case studies.

Culinary Incubator. www.culinaryincubator.com/maps.php.
This is an interactive map of commercial kitchens for use by small food businesses and cottage food producers.

CulinarySchools.org. www.culinaryschools.org.
This is a how-to guide for those wanting to know more about obtaining a culinary education. On this site, you will find degree information, career paths, and lists of top cooking schools and specialty schools by state, major, and career pathway.

edX. "The Ethics of Eating." www.edx.org/course/ethics-eating-cornellx-phil1440x.
This course explores the issues confronted when selecting or eating food. It involves philosophical, scientific, social, and industry approaches to the topic. It is offered by Cornell University in New York and brings many guest speakers and authors to the table in this discussion.

edX. "Feeding a Hungry Planet: Agriculture, Nutrition and Sustainability."
www.edx.org/course/feeding-a-hungry-planet-agriculture-nutrition-and-sustainability.
Offered by SDG Academy as an initiative of the UN Sustainable Development Solutions Network, this course aims to discuss sustainable agriculture as a means for developing better food systems.

edX. "Food for Thought." www.edx.org/course/food-for-thought.
This massive open online course, available from McGill University in Canada, focuses on the science and pseudoscience behind food choice and trends throughout history and how these have impacted human health and society. A certificate can be pursued for a low fee.

edX. "Nutrition and Disease."
www.edx.org/professional-certificate/wageningenx-nutrition-diseases.
This series of massive open online courses, available through the edx.org platform and offered by Wageningen University and Research from the Netherlands, focuses on the connectivity between food and health and food and disease. The two courses in this series, Nutrition and Cancer and Nutrition, Heart Disease, and Diabetes, can be taken separately for free or together for a paid certificate.

APPENDIX C: INTERACTIVE WEBSITES, TOOL KITS, AND MOOCS

edX. "Science and Cooking: From Haute Cuisine to Soft Matter Science."
www.edx.org/course/science-cooking-from-haute-cuisine-to-soft-matter-science-physics.
Offered by Harvard University in Cambridge, Massachusetts, this course deals with the science behind cooking, including basic kitchen chemistry, physics, and engineering.

edX. "The Science and Politics of the GMO." www.edx.org/course/science-politics-gmo-cornellx-gmo101x.
Brought to students by Cornell University in New York, this course explains the basics of genetic engineering and why it is such a contentious topic in today's food politics.

edX. "Sustainable Food Security." www.edx.org/xseries/food-security-sustainability.
This series of massive open online courses, available through the edx.org platform, covers the following topics: Food Access, Crop Production, and the Value of Systems. It is offered by Wageningen University and Research in the Netherlands. Each course can be taken separately for free or together for a paid certificate.

EPA. "Food Recovery Hierarchy." Sustainable Management of Food.
www.epa.gov/sustainable-management-food/food-recovery-hierarchy.
This site provides information on possible solutions such as source reduction, addressing hunger in humans and animals, industrial food scrap uses, and composting. There are a number of other tools available as well, including an excess food opportunities map and webinars on sustainable management of food topics.

FAO. www.fao.org.
The UNFAO was established in 1945 and has 197 member states. As a specialized agency of the United Nations, the UNFAO is tasked with discussing policy and providing information and resources relating to issues involving food, agriculture, forestry, fisheries, and nutrition. Their website is home to information about worldwide food security news, the international food safety conference, and the 2009 Declaration of the World Summit on Food Security. The UNFAO also hosts a podcast titled *Target: Zero Hunger*, which includes personal stories and frontline reporting.

Food and Agriculture Organization of the United Nations (FAO).
"The State of Food Security and Nutrition in the World." 2018.
www.fao.org/state-of-food-security-nutrition/en/.
This is an annual report prepared by the FAO; this year's key findings and discussions relate to hunger, obesity, climate resilience, water use and sanitation, and sustainable development.

FoodPantries.org. www.foodpantries.org.
This is a database that allows you to search by state to find a listing of local food pantries, soup kitchens, food banks, and other food help.

Foodtank—the Think Tank for Food. https://foodtank.com.
This is an excellent source of news and practical information about food movements and ideas. Foodtank regularly digs into topics such as the global food systems, environmental sustainability, government and policy, as well as local solutions. Find articles, podcast episodes, project reports, and event and summit information on their website.

Foodtank—the Think Tank for Food. "16 Apps Preventing Food Waste." September 16, 2018. https://foodtank.com/news/2018/09/apps-preventing-food-waste/.
Remember, roughly a third of all food produced for consumption ends up wasted. These apps, identified by Foodtank, can help cut back on the food that ends up in landfills.

McLaurin, Vatina. "Veganism: Eating Consciously and Compassionately." Library of Congress. 2011. www.loc.gov/rr/scitech/SciRefGuides/veganism.html.

National Farm to School Network. www.farmtoschool.org/our-network.
The National Farm to School Network is an information hub for connecting communities and schools with their local food and agriculture sector. Network resources include an interactive map that provides detailed information about each state, including state resources, policies, and individual case studies.

National Institute of Allergy and Infectious Diseases (NIAID). www.niaid.nih.gov.
Free pamphlets on food allergies and food allergy management can be ordered through their online publications portal.

National Network of Libraries of Medicine (NNLM). nnlm.gov.
The NNLM is a professional library network composed of academic, hospital, pharmaceutical, special, and public libraries as well as other health information centers. The NNLM connects its members to opportunities in continuing education, project funding, and policy development. Their mission is twofold: they work to advance medicine and public health, and they strive to improve public access to health information. The NNLM regularly offers free webinars on the topics of health information literacy, partnerships, and trusted resources. Many of these are easily available on the NNLM YouTube channel. They also offer resource demonstrations and other educational activities and programs, such as the certified health education specialization and the consumer health information specialization.

NNLM. "Health Literacy." https://nnlm.gov/initiatives/topics/health-literacy.
The NNLM provides definitions of health literacy alongside implications in consumer health, the health reference interview, and ethics. Their website also contains a breakdown of the skills needed for health literacy competence, initiatives to improve patient communication, and research findings on the impact of low health literacy. There is also information on best practices in evaluating health resources and websites.

Office of Disease Prevention and Health Promotion (DPHP). https://health.gov.
Within their "health literacy and communication" purview, the DPHP has several valuable resources aimed at health educators and practitioners. Health Literacy Online is an interactive educational module for professionals and practitioners, providing guidance on how to make medical practices and health-centric organizations more accessible for those struggling with health literacy and related literacies. Also available on the DPHP website, you can find the latest iteration of the National Action Plan to Improve Health Literacy (2010) as well as the Health Literate Care Model, a framework for coaching and developing health literacy.

Princeton University Library. "Cooking by the Book."
https://libguides.princeton.edu/c.php?g=394131&p=2677912.
This LibGuide not only provides a categorized listing of the cookbooks in the Princeton University Library but also has a comprehensive guide to other culinary collections and libraries across the country.

Seven Generations Ahead. "Zero Waste Schools Toolkit."
sevengenerationsahead.org/zero-waste/zero-waste-schools/.
The Zero Waste Schools initiative out of Illinois developed this tool kit. The tool kit is comprehensive, containing curriculum for K–5 aligned with Common Core and Next Generation Science Standards, school guides, signage for sorting, audit and measuring for impact guidelines, product guide, case studies, presentations, and more. This tool kit could easily be adapted for library use.

United States Department of Agriculture (USDA).
"Community Food Security Assessment Toolkit." USDA Economic Research Service.
www.ers.usda.gov/publications/pub-details/?pubid=43179.
This tool kit contains a number of useful pieces, including an overview of the process of data collection and analysis guidelines, a profile of community characteristics and food resources, and a breakdown of four different assessment types. Survey instruments and materials can also be found here.

USDA. "Food Access Research Atlas." USDA Economic Research Service. www.ers.usda.gov/data/fooddesert/.
This interactive atlas presents a spatial overview of food access based on the indicators of food security based on census tracts. Create and compare maps showing food access, view indicators for selected populations, and download census tract data.

USDA. "Food and Nutrition Service." www.fns.usda.gov.
Here, you can find the latest dietary guidelines as well as a comprehensive list and explanation of all federal food assistance programs, including Supplemental Nutrition Assistance Program (SNAP), Special Supplemental Nutrition Program for Women, Infants, and Children (WIC), Emergency Food Assistance Program (TEFAP), Commodity Supplemental Food Program (CSFP), Senior Farmer's Market Nutrition Program (SFMNP), Food Distribution Program on Indian Reservations (FDPIR), National School Lunch and Breakfast Programs (NSLP, SBP), Special Milk Program (SMP), and more.

USDA. "MyPlate." www.choosemyplate.gov.
This is an interactive website devoted to helping people make smart decisions about food. Features include dietary guidelines for Americans, 2015–20; the MyPlate, MyState food guide to local foods and teacher's tool kit; and a food group-customized plate planner.

USDA. "Where Can I Use SNAP EBT?" www.fns.usda.gov/snap/retailer-locator.
This is an interactive locator for finding retailers that accepts the Supplemental Nutrition Assistance Program (SNAP).

USDA Economic Research Service (ERS). www.ers.usda.gov.
This is a jackpot of economic reports related to the work of the USDA, including key reports such as *America's Diverse Family Farms 2018 Edition* and *Trends in the Adoption of Genetically Engineering Corn, Cotton, and Soybeans*. Other useful tools available here include the food environment atlas, USDA agricultural census maps, state of the industry reports, and a huge bank of data visualizations for all ERS reports.

WebstaurantStore. "Food Service Resources." www.webstaurantstore.com/food-service-resources.html.
This online retailer has a decent digital library of food-service how-to guides, business articles, and product reviews. Examples of content available free on their website include *Food Truck Buyers Guide 2018, Kitchen Equipment Every Restaurant Needs 2018, How to Clean and Organize a Commercial Fridge, Restaurant Equipment Certification Marks Explained*, and *Restaurant Labor Laws 2018*.

ABOUT THE CONTRIBUTORS

MEGAN AARANT is the teen services coordinator for the Chattahoochee Valley Libraries in Columbus, Georgia. In her eight-plus years with the system, her primary focus has been teen programming and outreach. Most recently she has worked with staff to create portable kits containing kitchen items so that cooking programs could be more affordable and accessible to branches system-wide.

STACY ALESI is the information desk librarian at Lynn University; prior to that, she was a research services librarian with the Palm Beach County Library System, where she created and facilitated the Cooking the Books discussion group. She created Stacy Alesi's BookBitch.com in 1998, is a professional reviewer (*Booklist, Library Journal*), presents webinars, speaks at various conferences, and is a self-proclaimed foodie.

DIANE ANNUNZIATO has been the assistant director / senior reference librarian at the Parker Memorial Library in Dracut, Massachusetts, for six years. Previously, she spent twelve years working at the Boxford Public Library in Boxford, Massachusetts. Both libraries have won top public relations awards from the Massachusetts Library Association for programming during her tenure.

LISA BREITHAUPT has always been interested in food. She grew up in Warren, Michigan, and lived in Lexington, Kentucky, for several years, where she obtained her master's degree in library and information science from the University of Kentucky. She moved to Cincinnati, Ohio, in 1994 and has been a librarian and branch manager for the Clermont County Library system for twenty-five years. She can also be seen in some of the local theater done in and around the city.

KATHLEEN CONNELLY-BROWN is the branch manager of Stilwell Public Library (Stilwell, OK), a branch of the Eastern Oklahoma District Library System. She has thirteen years of library experience. Cooking doesn't come naturally nor is it always taught at home, so she is glad to have the opportunity to teach these classes in a library setting.

DANIELLE COWARD is the outreach coordinator with the Elyria Public Library System in Ohio.

ABOUT THE CONTRIBUTORS

CATHERINE DEBERRY, MLS, is the adult services supervisor for the Somerset County Library System of New Jersey's Hillsborough Branch. DeBerry—a dedicated librarian for almost thirty years—is an innovative, cooperative thinker and is passionate about fostering adaptive and comprehensive library services for individuals with developmental disabilities, business professionals, lifelong learners, and other diverse populations.

APRIL GRIFFITH is the community engagement specialist librarian at the Eureka Springs Carnegie Public Library, where she works to spark curiosity and encourage the discovery of information and ideas through strategic outreach opportunities and creative programming. In addition to her passion for books and people, she loves to cook and has worked in commercial kitchens, baking and preparing food.

AUDREY L. JACOBS, MLIS, has been the young adult librarian at Shaker Heights Public Library for fifteen years. She first experienced the power of food to motivate, unite, and inspire young people while working her way through college in a myriad of food service–related jobs. Food brings us together.

LATRICIA MARKLE has always loved playing with food and books. As a children's librarian at the Tenafly Public Library in New Jersey, she takes every opportunity she can to share both with the children and teens in her community.

WENDY PEARSON is currently the director of adult services at the Richard Salter Storrs Library in Longmeadow, Massachusetts, where her passion for community engagement and innovative library programming keeps her hungry for ideas. Always pursuing the ultimate culinary experience, she regularly seeks out food-related programming for the library and has mastered the art of gormandizing while serving as an intern at the American Library in Paris.

LINDA PLEVAK, MLS, is a faculty instructor librarian at Northeast Lakeview College in Universal City, Texas. She formerly worked as the middle/upper school librarian at Saint Mary's Hall. There, she collaborated with Carol Parker-Mittal, teacher of art, who introduced her to International Edible Book Day. She enjoys creating vegetarian dishes with finds from local farmer's markets.

MELISSA SCHLOESSER is a creative senior library associate for the Pikes Peak Library District (PPLD). She has held many different positions during her six years of employment with PPLD. Prior to working for PPLD, Melissa completed a series of culinary art degrees from Pikes Peak Community College in Colorado and was employed in the culinary industry for ten years.

About the Contributors

KIM CHRISTIANSEN SIGLE worked as an elementary school librarian in Reston, Virginia, before becoming a library education specialist for Fairfax County Public Schools in Virginia. Although still learning to grow things, time spent with her four children and her background in outdoor education have led her to believe that with a garden and a library, you have everything you need.

NADINE BUCCILLI SPANO has more than ten years' experience as a librarian. She is the head of children's services at the Elmont Public Library. Before librarianship, Nadine was a marketing and promotions director in the private sector. She draws on that knowledge when serving the community with a special passion for enhancing visitor experiences and learning opportunities, such as with her Cooking with the Kids family program.

KARISA TASHJIAN serves as the director of education for the Providence Public Library. In this role, she leads the design and implementation of educational and workforce development programming across all ages that results in measurable engagement with and impact on the community. This project was a library-wide initiative including special collections, programs and exhibitions, information services, and the education departments.

CHRISTINA THURAIRATNAM is the head of reference and adult services at Holmes County District Public Library in Millersburg, Ohio. Although Christina cannot cook, she loves to bake, and her other food-related library programs include an edible book festival, a pie and cupcake bake-off, and a Peeps diorama contest.

LINDSEY TOMSU is currently the teen librarian at the Algonquin Area Public Library in Illinois. Previously, she was the teen librarian at the La Vista Public Library in Nebraska, where her teens created the idea of the bacon club, which ran successfully for a number of years before transforming into a baking club to teach teens basic cooking skills they would need in adulthood.

INDEX

A
Á la Carte food literacy project, 9
A la Rhody program, 68–69
Aarant, Megan, 59–60, 115
Accelerating Progress in Obesity Prevention (Institute of Medicine), 6
access, food, 4
"ACFEF Apprenticeships" (American Culinary Federation), 109
Ackerman-Leist, Philip, 16
ACS (American Community Survey), 35
action plan, 37
agriculture
    Backyard Chicken Basics program, 47–49
    changes needed for future of food, 17
Alesi, Stacy, 63–65, 115
Allenbaugh, Kay, 58
allergic reaction, 11–12
American Community Survey (ACS), 35
American Culinary Federation, 21–22, 109
American Dietetic Association, 3
American Planning Association, 37
The American Plate: A Culinary History in 100 Bites (O'Connell), 34
America's Test Kitchen, 42
An Unexpected Cookbook: The Unofficial Book of Hobbit Cookery (Oseland), 78
analysis, 36–37
anaphylaxis, 11
animal husbandry, 47–49
Annunziato, Diane, 47–49, 115
appendixes
    collection development, 97–102
    interactive websites, took kits, MOOCS, 109–114
    tools for community food assessment, 103–107
apprentice, 24
apprenticeships, 21–22
apps, 41
attendance, 85
    See also participants
autonomy, 12–13

B
Backyard Chicken Basics program, 47–49
bacon
    in dinner salad, 72
    Teen Bacon Club, 73–77
Bain, Carolyn, 51
Baines, Emily, 78
baking
    Cake Decorating for Teens, 54–55
    in cookbook club, 64
    Cupcake Wars program, 52–53
    Teen Baking Club, 73–77
    Your Baking Club Checklist, 71
Baking with Kids (Brooks), 42
Baltimarket, 15
Baltimore City Health Department's Virtual Supermarket Program, 15
Barclay, Jennifer, 69
bartender, 23
Beaupommier, Aurelia, 78
Benson, Jeffrey, 25
Benton Harbor Public Library, Michigan, 12
Bertlesen, C., 109
Beyond Meat, 17
Beyond the Chocolate War (Cormier), 58
Bittman, Mark, 13
Blaginin, Karla, 56
Blood, Bones & Butter (Hamilton), 64
Blood and Chocolate (Curtis Klause), 58
book club, 83
The Book Club Cookbook, Revised Edition: Recipes and Food for Thought from Your Book Club's Favorites Books and Authors (Gelman & Krupp), 69
The Book Lover's Cookbook: Recipes Inspired by Celebrated Works of Literature, and the Passages That Feature Them (Wenger), 69
books
    on business of food, 25
    chocolate-themed fiction booklist, 58
    cookbooks for kids, 42
    culinary collection development, 97–102
    fandom cookbooks, 78

INDEX

books *(cont.)*
    hot topics in food, 16
    International Edible Book Day, 49–51
    on science/sociology of food, 8
    travel memoir/world food culture collection, 51
Books and Cooks mobile kitchen program, 8
Books That Cook: The Making of a Literary Meal (Goldthwaite), 69
boucher (butcher), 24
boundaries, 32
Bourdain, Anthony
    Kitchen Confidential, 64
    A Moveable Feast, 51
Breithaupt, Lisa, 57–58, 115
brigade de cuisine
    brigade system for dining room, 24–26
    description of, 23
    roles within, 24
    table of, 24
Brooks, Leah, 42
Brown, Alton, 8
Brown, Sandra, 58
Brox, Jane, 49
Bucholz, Dinah, 78
Bureau of Labor Statistics, 21
business of food, 25
business specialist, 93
business topics, 98
Buttermilk Graffiti: A Chef's Journey to Discover America's New Melting-Pot Cuisine (Lee), 34

C

Cake Decorating for Teens, 54–55
Camden County Library System, New Jersey, 8
career
    culinary education/training, 21
    food career, fields/industries of, 22–23
Carl, Joanna, 58
Carle-Sanders, Theresa, 78
Catching Fire: How Cooking Made Us Human (Wrandman), 8
Centers for Disease Control and Prevention (CDC), 36
Chattanooga Public Library, 8
checklist, 71
chef
    education/training of, 21–22
    role of, 23
chef de cuisine (executive chef), 24
chef de partie (senior chef), 24
chef de rang, 25
chef de salle (floor manager), 24–25
chef de tourant, 23
chef de vin, 23
chef d'etage (captain), 25
chefs-resources.com, 109
chemicals, 14, 15
chickens
    Backyard Chicken Basics program, 47–49
    chicken stir-fry, 72
Chocolat (Harris), 58
chocolate
    chocolate-themed fiction booklist, 58
    Death by Chocolate program, 57–58
Chocolate Cat Caper (Hyde), 58
Chocolate Chip Cookie Murder (Hyde), 58
chocolate covered potato chips, 57–58
Chocolate for a Woman's Blessing (Allenbaugh), 58
Chocolate Frog Frame Up (Hyde), 58
Chocolate Puppy Puzzle: A Chocoholic Mystery (Carl), 58
The Chocolate War (Cormier), 58
choices, 12–13
church kitchens, 19
cicerone, 23
classes, 18
clean eating, 17
Clean Meat: How Growing Meat without Animals Will Revolutionize Dinner and the World (Shapiro), 16
cleanup, 85
Clearing Land: Legacies of an American Farm (Brox), 49
Clermont County Public Library, Ohio, 57–58
clubs
    cookbook clubs, 61–67
    Teen Bacon Club, 73–77
    Your Baking Club Checklist, 71
coding
    of community food assessment data, 36
    of research data, 36
collection
    business of food, 25
    chocolate-themed fiction booklist, 58
    fandom cookbooks, 78
    food allergies and, 12
    for food literacy program, 43, 44
    hot topics in food, 16
    literary dishes, 69
    science/sociology of food, 8
collection development
    business topics, 98
    cooking methods, 98–99
    cuisine styles, 99
    diets, 99–100

INDEX **121**

equipment, 100
food/drink, types of, 101–102
nutrition topics, 100–101
subject lists, 97–98
Western meals/menu categories, 102
world cuisines, 101
Columbus Public Library, Chattahoochee Valley Libraries, Georgia, 59–60
commis (line cook), 24
commodity foods, 70
community
   Eat Play Grow program for, 88–89
   Edible Education Garden and, 81, 82
   Food ED and, 92
   food literacy in libraries and, 7, 8–9, 95
   interest in local food system, 30
   Recipe Club and, 65, 66, 67
Community Action Partnership, 36
Community Commons
   Maps and Data, 35
   website, 110
community food assessment
   action plans/indicators, 37
   benefits of, 29
   benefits of/process of, xi
   conducting, 35–37
   primary data, 32–33
   questions for, 31–32
   readiness, assessment of, 29–31
   road-trip inspired books, 34
   secondary data, 33
   steps of, 32
   team members, 31
   tools for, 103–107
   work plan, 33–34
Community Food Assessment: Laying the Foundation, 104–105
Community Food Assessment: Readiness Questionnaire, 103
Community Food Assessment: Work Plan Template, 106–107
Community Food Project Evaluation Handbook (National Research Center), 37
"Community Food Security Assessment Toolkit" (USDA), 113
Community Food Security Coalition, 36
Community Food Strategies website, 37
community forums, 35
community gardens
   Edible Education Garden, 80–82
   enabling, 9
   food deserts and, 15
   at libraries, 18

community partnerships, 55–56
community-supported agriculture (CSA), 49
The Complete Cookbook for Young Chefs (America's Test Kitchen), 42
The Complete Idiot's Guide to Starting a Food Truck Business (Philips), 25
Conant, Scott, 65
Connelly-Brown, Kathleen
   information about, 115
   Teen Cooking Classes, 69–73
consumer impact, 12–13
cook
   education/training of, 21–22
   role of, 23
Cookbook Club at Storrs Library, 61–62
cookbook clubs
   Cookbook Club at Storrs Library, 61–62
   Cooking the Books, 63–65
   Recipe Club, 65–67
cookbooks
   collection development, 99–102
   fandom, list of, 78
   for kids, 42
   for Teen Baking Club, 75
Cooked: A Natural History of Transformation (Pollan), 8
cooking
   from Edible Education Garden, 81
   Teen Maker Club, 82–85
   Your Baking Club Checklist, 71
"Cooking by the Book" (Princeton University Library), 113
cooking class
   Cake Decorating for Teens, 54–55
   Cooking with the Kids, 85–87
   Death by Chocolate program, 57–58
   Getting Started with Your Instant Pot program, 53–54
   Mobile Kitchen for, 77, 79–80
   Teen Cooking Classes, 69–73
   Teen Maker Club, 82–85
cooking shows
   Cupcake Wars program, 52–53
   Ramen Iron Chef program, 59–60
   teen cooking competition, 77
Cooking the Books cookbook club, 63–65
Cooking up a Business: Lessons from Food Lovers Who Turned Their Passion into a Career— and How You Can Too (Hofstetter), 25
Cooking with the Kids, 85–87
cooking methods, 98–99
cordero al palo, ix
core questions, 31–34

Cormier, Robert, 58
Coron, Beatrice, 49
corporations, 14
cost
    of Cooking with the Kids program, 87
    of Eat Play Grow program, 89
    of Teen Cooking Classes, 73
Coward, Danielle, 88–89, 115
crackers, flavored, 75–76
Cravings (Teigen), 64
Crazy as Chocolate (Hyde), 58
Croce, E., 25
CSA (community-supported agriculture), 49
cuisine styles, 99
cuisiner (station cook), 24
culinary arts
    brigade de cuisine, 23–26
    collection development, 97–102
    fields/industries, 22–23
    job outlook for chefs/head cooks, 21
    resources on, 25
    terminology, 23
    top culinary schools in U.S., 22
    training/education, 21–22
culinary education
    Cake Decorating for Teens, 54–55
    Mobile Kitchen for, 77, 79–80
    overview of, 21–22
    Teen Maker Club, 82–85
Culinary Incubator website, 110
Culinary Institute of America, 42
culinary literacy
    definition of, 6
    preparation domain of food literacy, 4–5
"Culinary Literacy: A Toolkit for Public Libraries" (Free Library of Philadelphia), 8
Culinary Literacy Center, Philadelphia Free Public Library, 7–8
culinary schools, 22
CulinarySchools.org, 110
Cultural Revolution Cookbook (Gong), 83
culture
    Dia de los Muertos Community Altar program, 55–56
    Ramen Iron Chef program, 59–60
Cupcake Wars program, 52–53
curanto en hoyo, ix
Curtis, Andrea, 16
Curtis Klause, Annette, 58

D

D'Amato, Barbara, 58
Daniels, Patricia, 42

data
    action plan after collection of, 37
    from community food assessment, 32–33
    community food assessment, conducting, 35–37
Davis, Robin, 78
Dawson, Paul, 8
Death by Chocolate (McKevett), 58
Death by Chocolate program, 57–58
Death Is Semi-Sweet (Temple), 58
DeBerry, Catherine
    information about, 116
    Recipe Club, 65–67
decisions, 4
Declaration of Human Rights (UN), 14
Deep Run Roots: Stories and Recipes from My Corner of the South (Howard), 64
degrees, 22
Delicious (Reichl), 64
demi chef, 24
demi-chef de rang (table busser), 25
design, 39–40
Devane, Rhett, 58
Dewey Decimal System summaries, 97
Dia de los Muertos Community Altar program, 55–56
Dichos de la Casa, 55–56
Did You Just Eat That? Two Scientists Explore Double-Dipping, the Five-Second Rule, and Other Food Myths in the Lab (Dawson & Sheldon), 8
diets
    collection development, 99–100
    overview of, 17–18
    Teen Cooking Classes, 69–73
Diners, Drive-Ins and Dives: The Funky Finds in Flavortown: America's Classic Joints and Killer Comfort Food (Fieri), 34
Dining In (Roman), 64
dining room, brigade system for, 24–26
dinner salad, 72
dishes, literary, 69
Doctor Who: The Official Cookbook: 40 Wibbly-Wobbly Timey-Wimey Recipes (Farrow), 78
Dodge, Hillary, ix–x
Doherty, Tom, 48
Dracut Agricultural Commission, 48
"Dracut Reads and Eats 2018!" program, 48–49
Dreamweavers storytelling troupe, 57
drinks, 101–102
Dunn, Rob, 16
Dying for Chocolate (Mott Davidson), 58

E

Eat & Move-O-Matic (Learning Games Lab), 41
Eat Drink Vote: An Illustrated Guide to Food Politics (Nestle), 16
Eat Play Grow, 88–89
Eat Your Greens, Reds, Yellows, and Purples: Children's Cookbook (Mitchem, Love, & King), 42
Eating across America: A Foodie's Guide to Food Trucks, Street Food and the Best Dish in Each State (Patterson), 34
eating domain, 5
Eating Words: A Norton Anthology of Food Writing (Gilbert et al.), 51
EatPlayGrow Curriculum, 88–89
Economic Research Service (ERS), 114
Edible Book Day (EBD), 49–51
Edible Education Garden, 80–82
education
    See culinary education
edX, 110, 111
Eight Flavors: The Untold Story of American Cuisine (Lohman), 34
Elmont Public Library, Hempstead, New York, 85–87
Elyria City School District, 88–89
Elyria Public Library System (EPLS), 88–89
Entrepreneur Media, 25
Environmental Protection Agency, 111
environmental scans, 36
equipment, 100
    See also kitchen equipment
equipment-based cookbooks, 100
ERS (Economic Research Service), 114
Escoffier, Georges Auguste, 23
Esquivel, Laura, 58
essential collections
    American Road Trip, 34
    business of food, 25
    cookbooks for kids, 42
    fandom cookbooks, 78
    hot topics in food, 16
    literary dishes, titles on, 69
    science/sociology of food, 8
    travel memoir/world food culture, 51
ethics
    food ethics, 12–13
    of meat production/processing, 17
"The Ethics of Eating" (edX), 110
Eureka Springs Carnegie Public Library, Illinois, 82–85
Evershed, Richard, 16
Everyday Gourmet series, 64
The Evolved Eater: A Quest to Eat Better, Live Better, and Change the World (Taranto), 16
Ewing Marion Kauffman Foundation, 92

F

Fair Food: Growing a Healthy, Sustainable Food System for All (Hesterman), 16
fair trade, 13
fairness, 12–13
FALCPA (Food Allergen Labeling and Consumer Protection Act), 12
family
    Cooking with the Kids program and, 85–87
    in Cupcake Wars program, 52–53
fandom cookbooks, 78
FAO (Food and Agriculture Organization of the United Nations), 14, 111
farm to table, 17
Farrow, Joanna, 78
A Feast of Ice and Fire: The Official Game of Thrones Companion Cookbook (Monroe-Cassel), 78
"Feeding a Hungry Planet: Agriculture, Nutrition and Sustainability" (edX), 110
Feigenbaum, Michael, 54–55
Fictitious Dishes: An Album of Literature's Most Memorable Meals (Fried), 69
Fieri, Guy, 34
Fifty Shades of Chicken: A Parody in a Cookbook (Fowler), 78
Fizzy's Lunch Lab (PBS), 41
Flavor Lab, 8
focus groups, 35
FocusOn: Food series, 13
food
    as basic human need, 3
    Edible Education Garden, 80–82
    International Edible Book Day, 49–51
    titles on science/sociology of, 8
    types of food/drink, 101–102
    world food culture collection, 51
"Food Access Research Atlas" (USDA), 114
Food Allergen Labeling and Consumer Protection Act (FALCPA), 12
food allergies
    dealing with in food literacy program, 43
    discussion of in Teen Baking Club, 75
    food intolerances vs., 11–12
Food and Agriculture Organization of the United Nations (FAO), 14, 111
"Food and Nutrition Service" (USDA), 114
Food and Wine Tourism, 2nd Edition (Croce), 25

food business
    Food ED, 90–94
    resources on, 25
food choices, 5
food deserts
    community gardens and, 80
    description of, 14–15
    food rescue efforts in, 19
food distributor, 43
Food ED, 90–94
food ethics, 12–13
"Food for Thought" (edX), 110
food fraud, 13
Food Journeys of a Lifetime: 500 Extraordinary Places to Eat around the Globe (National Geographic), 51
food justice, 14
The Food Lab (Lopez-Alt), 64
food labels, 4
Food Lit: A Reader's Guide to Epicurean Nonfiction (Stoeger), 97
food literacy
    collection development, 97–102
    definition, reason it matters, 6–7
    definition of, 3–4
    domains of, 4–5
    impact on communities, 95
    in libraries, 7–9
    related terms, 6
food literacy programs/services
    overview of book's coverage of, xi–xii
    program logistics, 40, 43–44
    questions for, 39–40
    stories as examples of, x
food literacy quick-start guide
    cookbooks for kids, 42
    foodie websites/apps for kids, 41
    program logistics, 40, 43–44
    questions about food literacy program, 39–40
Food Lover's Guide to the World: Experience the Great Global Cuisines (Bain), 51
food miles, 13
food movements
    diets, popular, 17–18
    food allergies/intolerances, 11–12
    food ethics/food system, 12–13
    food security/food deserts, 13–15
    food waste/food rescue, 18–19
    GMOs/future of food, 15–17
    hot topics in food, 16
Food Network, 52

Food on Wheels: The Complete Guide to Starting a Food Truck, Food Cart, or Other Mobile Food Business (Lewis), 25
food pantry, 9, 19
food programs
    Cooking with the Kids, 85–87
    in libraries, x
    See also programs
"Food Recovery Hierarchy" (EPA), 111
food rescue, 15, 19
food resources, 4
food safety
    See safety
food security
    "Community Food Security Assessment Toolkit" (USDA), 113
    food deserts and, 14–15
    overview of, 13–14
"Food Service Resources" (WebstaurantStore), 114
food sovereignty, 14
food system
    community interest in local, 30
    elements of, 3
    food ethics and, 12–13
    food sovereignty and, 14
    future of food, 16–17
    GMOs in, 15–16
    terms related to, 13
The Food Truck Handbook: Start, Grow, and Succeed in the Mobile Food Business (Weber), 25
Food Truck Workshop, 92
food waste, 18–19
food/drink, types, 101–102
FoodPantries.org, 112
food-service industry, 22
foodshed, 13
Foodtank, 112
foodwork, 6
A Fork in the Road: Tales of Food, Pleasure and Discovery on the Road (Oseland), 51
Fort Hays State University, Kansas, 9
Fowler, F. L., 78
Freeman, Danyelle, 51
FreeRice, 41
The French Laundry Cookbook (Keller), 63–64
French Silk (Brown), 58
Fried, Dinah, 69
"From Soup to Nuts"
    culinary arts, primer to field of, 21–26
    food literacy, 3–9

food movements, 11–19
  overview of, xi
fruits, 80–82
The Fuzzy Pig, 90

G

garde manger (keeper of the food), 24
gardening
  in Backyard Chicken Basics program, 47, 48
  community gardens, 9, 15, 18
  Edible Education Garden, 80–82
Garten, Ina
  cookbooks by, 64
  Make It Ahead, 62
Gather 'Round the Table (Dodge)
  origins of, ix–x
  overview of, xi–xii
The Geek's Cookbook: Easy Recipes Inspired by Pokémon, Harry Potter, Star Wars, and More! (Lecomte), 78
The Geeky Chef Cookbook (Reeder), 78
The Geeky Chef Drinks: Unofficial Cocktail Recipes from Game of Thrones, Legend of Zelda, Star Trek, and More (Reeder), 78
Gelman, Judy, 69
genetically modified organisms (GMOs)
  future of food and, 16–17
  from green revolution, 14
  issues of, 15–16
Getting Started with Your Instant Pot program, 53–54
Getting Your Specialty Food Product onto Store Shelves: The Ultimate Wholesale How-to Guide for Artisan Food Companies. (Lewis), 25
Gherkins and Tomatoes website, 109
Gilbert, Sandra, 51
gingerbread house-making program, 86
global food ethics, 13
GMOs
  See genetically modified organisms
Goldthwaite, Melissa, 69
Gong, Sasha, 83
Good Food, Great Business: How to Take Your Artisan Food Idea from Concept to Marketplace (Wyshak), 25
Goudge, Eileen, 58
granola bars, 72
grant
  for Eat Play Grow program, 88
  Healthy Living grant, 77, 79
  for Mobile Kitchen, 77, 79

Grant, Amanda, 42
Great American Eating Experiences: Local specialties, favorite restaurants, food festivals, diners, roadside stands, and more (National Geographic), 34
green revolution, 14
Greenwich Library, Connecticut, 13
Gresham, Douglas, 78
Griffith, April
  information about, 116
  Teen Maker Club, 82–85
grillardin (grill chef), 24
Gross, Suzanne, 42
Gulp: Adventures on the Alimentary Canal (Roach), 8
Gwinnett County Public Library, Lawrenceville, Georgia, 55–56

H

Hahn, Diane, 65–67
Hamilton, Gabrielle, 64
Hammer, Melina, 42
Harris, Joanne, 58
Have Fork, Will Travel (Wolf), 25
health literacy, 6
"Health Literacy" (NNLM), 113
healthy food
  Cooking with the Kids, 85–87
  Eat Play Grow, 88–89
  Edible Education Garden, 80–82
  Teen Cooking Classes, 69–73
Healthy Living grant, 77, 79
The Help Yourself Cookbook for Kids: 60 Easy Plant-Based Recipes Kids Can Make to Stay Healthy and Save the Earth (Roth), 42
Hesterman, Oran, 16
high school students, 82
history, 68–69
Hoffberg, Judith, 49
Hofstetter, Rachel, 25
Holmes County Public Library, 53–54
Homemade for Sale: How to Set Up and Market a Food Business from Your Home Kitchen (Kivirist), 25
Honest Pretzels: And 64 Other Amazing Recipes for Cooks Ages 8 and Up (Katzen), 42
hostess, 25–26
hot topics in food, 16
house specials
  Cookbook Club at Storrs Library, 61–62
  Cooking the Books, 63–65
  Cooking with the Kids, 85–87

house specials *(cont.)*
    description of, xii
    Eat Play Grow, 88–89
    Edible Education Garden, 80–82
    fandom cookbooks, 78
    Food Ed, 90–94
    literary dishes, titles on, 69
    Mobile Kitchen, 77, 79–80
    Recipe Club, 65–67
    On the Table exhibition, 68–69
    Teen Bacon Club, 73–77
    Teen Cooking Classes, 69–73
    Teen Maker Club, 82–85
    Your Baking Club Checklist, 71
Howard, Vivian, 64
Hughes, Meredith, 16
Hyde, Elisabeth, 58
hygiene
    in mobile kitchen, 80
    in Teen Baking Club, 75, 76

I

In Defense of Food: An Eater's Manifesto (Pollan), 16
indicators, 37
Instant Pot, 53–54
Institute of Medicine, 6
International Edible Book Day, 49–51
intolerances, 11–12
Issa's Edible Adventures website, 41

J

Jacobs, Audrey L., 54–55, 116
Japanese culture, 59–60
Jennifer, Lewis, 25
judges, 50

K

kalapulka (beef and pork stew), ix
Karmel, Annabel, 42
Katzen, Mollie, 42
Keller, Thomas, 63–64
Keystone Empowers You, 89
Keystone Local School District, 88–89
Kid Chef: The Foodie Kids Cookbook: Healthy Recipes and Culinary Skills for the New Cook in the Kitchen (Hammer), 42
King, Dave, 42
Kiple, Kenneth, 8
kitchen
    mobile kitchen, 77, 79–80
    skills, 4–5

Kitchen Confidential (Bourdain), 64
kitchen equipment
    equipment-based cookbooks, 100
    for mobile kitchen, 79–80
    purchase of, 43
    for Teen Baking Club, 75
    for Teen Maker Club, 83–84
    Your Baking Club Checklist, 71
Kitchens of the Great Midwest (Stradal), 64
Kivirist, Lisa, 25
knives
    safety of food literacy program, 40, 43
    safety with, 75
    in Teen Cooking Class, 72
Korean cooking, 49
Koslow, Christopher, 64
Krupp, Vicki, 69

L

La Vista Public Library, La Vista, Nebraska, 73–77
labor market information (LMI), 92
Lake Anne Elementary School, Reston, Virginia, 80–82
Latin American heritage, 55–56
Learning Games Lab, 41
Lecomte, Liguori, 78
Lee, Edward, 34
Let the Meatballs Rest: And Other Stories about Food and Culture (Montanari), 51
librarians
    business resources for small business owner, 93
    International Edible Book Day, collaboration for, 49–51
libraries
    diets, collection/programs about, 18
    Edible Education Garden, 80–82
    food assessments, value in, 29
    food ethics and, 12–13
    food literacy in, 7–9
    food programs, demand for, 61
    food programs in, ideas about, xii
    food rescue efforts of, 19
    See also collection
Library of Congress subject headings, 98
life expectancy, 70
Like Water for Chocolate (Esquivel), 58
literacy, 6
    See also food literacy
Literary Feast: Recipes Inspired by Novels, Poems and Plays (Barclay), 69

A Literary Tea Party: Blends and Treats for Alice, Bilbo, Dorothy, Jo, and Book Lovers Everywhere (Walsh), 69
Livewell Colorado Data Collection website, 36
local history, 68–69
Lohman, Sarah, 34
Lopez-Alt, J. Kenji, 64
Love, Carrie, 42
low-calorie diet, 17
low-carb diet, 18
low-fat diet, 17
Lucy's Sweet Surrender, 54–55

M

The Madhatter's Guide to Chocolate (Devane), 58
maître d' (general manager), 24
Make It Ahead (Garten), 62
maker club, 82–85
makeup, of food product, 4
marketing
 See promotion
Markle, Latricia, 52–53, 116
Massive Open Online Courses (MOOCS), 109–114
MasterChef Junior Cookbook: Bold Recipes and Essential Techniques to Inspire Young Cooks (McLachlan), 42
McGee, Harold, 8
McKevett, G. A., 58
McLachlan, Clay, 42
McLaurin, Vatina, 112
McNamee, Gregory, 8
meat
 alternatives to, 17
 Teen Bacon Club, 73–77
Mediterranean diet, 18
Mid-Continent Public Library, Kansas City, Missouri, 90–94
mise en place concept, 23
Missoula Public Library, 8
Mitchem, James, 42
mobile kitchen
 Books and Cooks mobile kitchen program, 8
 creation of, 77, 79–80
 Food ED, 90–94
Mom and Me Cookbook (Karmel), 42
monoculture environment, 15
Monroe-Cassel, Chelsea, 78
Montanari, Massimo, 51
MOOCS (Massive Open Online Courses), 109–114
Mott Davidson, Diana, 58

A Moveable Feast (Bourdain), 51
A Moveable Feast: Ten Millennia of Food Globalization (Kiple), 8
Moveable Feasts: The History, Science, and Lore of Food (McNamee), 8
"MyPlate" (USDA), 114
Myrick, Richard, 25

N

National Farm to School Network, 112
National Geographic, 34, 51
National Institute of Allergy and Infectious Diseases (NIAID), 12, 112
National Institutes of Health, 88
National Network of Libraries of Medicine (NNLM), 112, 113
National Research Center, 37
Native Americans, 69–73
Nestle, Marion, 16
Never Out of Season: How Having the Food We Want When We Want It Threatens Our Food Supply and Our Future (Dunn), 16
A New Napa Cuisine (Koslow), 64
New Policeman (Thompson), 83
newsletters, 64
NIAID (National Institute of Allergy and Infectious Diseases), 12, 112
NNLM (National Network of Libraries of Medicine), 112, 113
No Half Measures: A Life in Wine, Food and Travel (Benson), 25
no-food policy, 39
Northern Onondaga Public Library, 15
Nosrat, Samin, 8
The Nourishing Traditions Cookbook for Children: Teaching Children to Cook the Nourishing Traditions Way (Gross et al.), 42
"Nutrition and Disease" (edX), 110
nutrition literacy, 6
nutrition topics, 100–101

O

objectives, 30
O'Connell, Libby, 34
Of Course You Know That Chocolate Is a Vegetable and Other Stories (D'Amato), 58
Office of Disease Prevention and Health Promotion (DPHP), 113
The Official Narnia Cookbook: Food from the Chronicles of Narnia by C. S. Lewis (Gresham), 78
ofrendas (remembrance altars), 56

Ohio State University Extension Office, Holmes County, Ohio, 54
Olmsted, Larry, 16
The Omnivore's Dilemma: A Natural History of Four Meals (Pollan), 8
On Food and Cooking: The Science and Lore of the Kitchen (McGee), 8
On the Table exhibition, 68–69
1,000 Foods to Eat before You Die: A Food Lover's Life List (Sheraton), 51
"Online Cookbooks and Other Culinary Materials: Sources" (Bertlesen), 109
Oseland, Chris-Rachel, 78
Oseland, James, 51
Ottawa Public Library, 9
Outlander Kitchen: The Official Outlander Companion Cookbook (Carle-Sanders), 78
oven, 75

P

Paleolithic diet, 18
parents
    Cooking with the Kids program and, 85–87
    Eat Play Grow program and, 89
    as volunteers in Edible Education Garden, 81
Parker Memorial Library, Dracut, Massachusetts, 47–49
Parker-Mittal, Carol, 49–51
participants
    in Eat Play Grow program, 89
    in food literacy program, 40
Patagonia, 13
pâtissier (pastry chef), 24
Patterson, Daymon, 34
PBS, 41
Pearson, Wendy, 61–62, 116
Perelman, Deb, 64
Perry, Morgan, 90–94
Philadelphia Free Public Library, 7–8
Philips, Alan, 25
Phillips, Ethan, 78
Pikes Peak Library District, Colorado Springs, Colorado
    Mobile Kitchen, 77, 79–80
    seed library, 8–9
pizza waffles, 76
plan
    action plan, 37
    Community Food Assessment: Work Plan Template, 106–107
    work plan for community food assessment, 33–34

planning and management domain
    components of/application examples, 5
    of International Edible Books Day, 50
    subcategories within, 4
Plants vs. Meats: The Health, History, and Ethics of What We Eat (Hughes), 16
Plevak, Linda, 49–51, 116
poissonier (fish cook), 24
Pollan, Michael
    Cooked: A Natural History of Transformation, 8
    In Defense of Food: An Eater's Manifesto, 16
    The Omnivore's Dilemma: A Natural History of Four Meals, 8
potager (stocks, soups, and stews cook), 24
POTATO Club, 74
potlucks, 61–62
PPL (Providence Public Library), 68–69
preparation domain, 4, 5
presenter
    for Backyard Chicken Basics program, 48
    for Getting Started with Your Instant Pot program, 54
    for Recipe Club, 66, 67
Pretend Soup and Other Real Recipes: A Cookbook for Preschoolers and Up (Katzen), 42
primary data
    of community food assessment, 32–33
    community food assessment, conducting, 35–36
Princeton University Library, 113
prizes, 50, 51
programs
    Backyard Chicken Basics program, 47–49
    Cake Decorating for Teens, 54–55
    Cookbook Club at Storrs Library, 61–62
    Cooking the Books, 63–65
    Cooking with the Kids, 85–87
    Cupcake Wars program, 52–53
    Death by Chocolate program, 57–58, 59–60
    Dia de los Muertos Community Altar program, 55–56
    Eat Play Grow, 88–89
    Edible Education Garden, 80–82
    fandom cookbooks, 78
    Food ED, 90–94
    International Edible Book Day, 49–51
    Mobile Kitchen, 77, 79–80
    Recipe Club, 65–67
    On the Table exhibition, 68–69
    Teen Bacon Club, 73–77
    Teen Cooking Classes, 69–73

Teen Maker Club, 82–85
Your Baking Club Checklist, 71
promotion
    of Eat Play Grow program, 89
    of International Edible Books Day, 50
    of A la Rhody, 69
"The Proof Is in the Pudding"
    house specials, 61–94
    overview of, xii
    short orders, 47–60
"pro-tips," 83
Providence Public Library (PPL), 68–69
Public Libraries (magazine), x

Q

quality of food, 4
quality outcomes, 4–5
questionnaires, 36, 103
questions
    about library food literacy program, 39–40
    for assessment of readiness for community food assessment, 29–31
    for community food assessment, 31–32
    for community food assessment work plan, 33–34
Quinn, Sue, 51

R

Ratio: The Simple Codes behind the Craft of Everyday Cooking (Ruhlman), 8
readiness
    for community food assessment, 29–31
    Community Food Assessment: Readiness Questionnaire, 103
reading, 49–51
Real Food/Fake Food: Why You Don't Know What You're Eating and What You Can Do about It (Olmsted), 16
Rebuilding the Foodshed: How to Create Local, Sustainable, and Secure Food Systems (Ackerman-Leist), 16
Recipe Club, 65–67
Recipe for Success: An Insider's Guide to Bringing Your Natural Good to Market (Steinberg), 25
recipes
    Cookbook Club at Storrs Library and, 62
    in Cooking the Books, 64
    reading, 75
    Recipe Club, 65–67
    for Teen Baking Club, 74, 75–76
    in Teen Maker Club, 84

recruiting, 34
Reeder, Cassandra, 78
"regularity," 14
Reichl, Ruth, 51, 64
related terms
    See terminology
relief cook, 23
religion-based diets, 18
report, 37
resources
    on business of food, 25
    for community food assessment, 31, 36
    cookbooks for kids, 42
    fandom cookbooks, 78
    foodie websites/apps for kids, 41
    hot topics in food, 16
    road-trip inspired books, 34
    on science/sociology of food, 8
    sharing with Food ED, 91–94
    travel memoir/world food culture collection, 51
    work plan for community food assessment, 33
    See also appendixes
restaurant cookbooks, 64–65
results, of community food assessment, 31
Rhode Island, 68–69
Richard Salter Storrs Library, Longmeadow, Massachusetts, 61–62
Richmond Public Library, California, 8
"right to food," 14
right-to-farm community, 47, 48
Ripert, Eric, 64
Roach, Mary, 8
Roadfood, 10th Edition: An Eaters Guide to More than 1,000 of the Best Local Hot Spots and Hidden Gems across America (Stern), 34
road-trip inspired books, 34
Rockridge University Press, 78
roles, 24–26
Roman, Alison, 64
roosters, 48
Roth, Ruby, 42
rotisseur (roast chef), 24
Ruhlman, Michael, 8
Running a Food Truck for Dummies (Myrick), 25
Russell, Harriet, 42

S

safety
    in Cooking with the Kids program, 86–87
    in food literacy program, 40, 43
    in mobile kitchen, 80

safety *(cont.)*
    in Teen Baking Club, 76
    in Teen Cooking Classes, 72, 73
Saint Mary's Hall, San Antonio, Texas, 49–51
Salt, Fat, Acid, Heat: Mastering the Elements of Good Cooking (Nosrat), 8
Samuelsson, Marcus, 64
sanitation, 40, 80
    See also hygiene
saucier (sauté chef), 24
Saul, Nick, 16
Save Me the Plums (Reichl), 51
Scarpetta (restaurant), 65
Schloesser, Melissa
    information about, 117
    on Mobile Kitchen, 77, 79–80
science, 8
"Science and Cooking: From Haute Cuisine to Soft Matter Science" (edX), 111
"The Science and Politics of the GMO" (edX), 111
Scone with the Wind: Cakes and Bakes with a Literary Twist (Sponge), 69
SCORE mentors, 92–93
secondary data, 33, 35
security
    See food security
seed libraries, 8–9
Seeds of Resistance: The Fight to Save Our Food Supply (Shapiro), 16
selection domain, 4, 5
self-awareness, 5
ServeSafe, 40
Seven Generations Ahead, 113
Shaker Heights Public Library, Ohio, 54–55
Shapiro, Mark, 16
Shapiro, Paul, 16
sharing, 37
Sheldon, Brian, 8
Sheraton, Mimi, 51
short orders
    Backyard Chicken Basics program, 47–49
    Cake Decorating for Teens, 54–55
    Cupcake Wars program, 52–53
    Death by Chocolate program, 57–58, 59–60
    description of, xii
    Dia de los Muertos Community Altar program, 55–56
    Getting Started with Your Instant Pot program, 53–54
    International Edible Book Day, 49–51
    travel memoir/world food culture collection, 51
short-order cook, 23

Sigle, Kim Christiansen, 80–82, 116
The Silver Spoon for Children: Favorite Italian Recipes (Russell & Grant), 42
Simpson, Abby, 77
"16 Apps Preventing Food Waste" (Foodtank), 112
small business program, 90–94
A Smart Girl's Guide: Cooking: How to Make Food for Your Friends, Your Family and Yourself (Daniels), 42
The Smitten Kitchen Cookbook (Perelman), 64
smoothies, 71–72
The Snacking Dead: A Parody in a Cookbook (Walker), 78
SNAP (Supplemental Nutrition Assistance Program), 114
social eating, 5, 6
social good, 7
sociology, 8
Somerset County Library System of New Jersey (SCLSNJ), 65–67
sommelier, 23
Sorting the Beef from the Bull: The Science of Food Fraud Forensics (Evershed & Temple), 16
sous chef (second chef), 24
space
    for Cooking with the Kids program, 86–87
    for food literacy program, 40
Spano, Nadine Buccilli, 85–87, 117
Sponge, Miss Victoria, 69
Square One Small Business Services, 90–94
staff-led meetings, 66
stakeholder interviews, 35
stakeholders, 30, 31
Star Trek Cookbook (Phillips), 78
Start Your Own Food Truck Business: Cart Trailer Kiosk Standard and Gourmet Trucks Mobile Catering Bustaurant (Entrepreneur Media), 25
Start Your Own Specialty Food Business: Your Step-by-Step Startup Guide to Success (Entrepreneur Media), 25
State Library of Ohio, 88
"The State of Food Security and Nutrition in the World" (FAO), 111
Steinberg, Abigail, 25
Stern, Jane, 34
Stilwell Public Library Friends Society, 70
Stilwell Public Library, Oklahoma, 69–73
Stoeger, Melissa Brackney, 97
The Stop: How the Fight for Good Food Transformed a Community and Inspired a Movement (Saul & Curtis), 16

stories, 63
Stradal, J. Ryan, 64
Stuart, Tristam, 16
students, 80–82
subject experts, 31
subject lists, 97–98
Such Devoted Sisters (Goudge), 58
Supplemental Nutrition Assistance Program (SNAP), 114
supplies
    for Eat Play Grow program, 88
    for mobile kitchen, 79–80
    for Teen Baking Club, 75
    for Teen Maker Club, 83–84
surveys, 36
Sushi Singularity, 17
"Sustainable Food Security" (edX), 111
swing cook, 23

T

TAB (teen advisory board), 74
table exhibition, 68–69
TAG (teen advisory group), 83
"Take the Cake"
    community food assessment, 29–37
    food literacy quick-start guide, 39–44
    overview of, xi
Taranto, Nick, 16
Target: Zero Hunger (UNFAO podcast), 111
Tashjian, Karisa, 68–69, 117
teachers, 49–51
team
    for community food assessment, 31, 35–37
    in Cupcake Wars program, 52–53
    work plan for community food assessment, 33–34
technical school, 21–22
teen advisory board (TAB), 74
teen advisory group (TAG), 83
Teen Bacon Club, 73–77
Teen Baking Club, 73–77
Teen Cooking Classes, 69–73
Teen Maker Club, 82–85
teens
    Cake Decorating for Teens, 54–55
    Ramen Iron Chef program for, 59–60
    Teen Bacon Club, 73–77
    Teen Cooking Classes, 69–73
    Teen Maker Club, 82–85
Teigen, Chrissy, 64
Temple, Lou, 58
Temple, Nicola, 16

Tenafly Public Library, New Jersey, 52–53
terminology
    of culinary arts, 23
    of food ethics, 13
    of food insecurity, 14
    of food issues, 11
32 Yolks (Ripert), 64
This Is My Food—Nutrition for Kids (urbn pockets), 41
Thompson, Kate, 83
Thurairatnam, Christina, 53–54, 117
The Tickle Fingers Toddler Cookbook: Hands-On Fun in the Kitchen for 1 To 4s (Woolmer), 42
Tiger Food Exchange, 9
time line, 33
tips, 50, 83
Toca Kitchen (Toca Boca), 41
The Toddler Cookbook (Karmel), 42
Tomsu, Lindsey, 73–77, 117
tools
    for community food assessment, 103–107
    interactive websites, took kits, and MOOCS, 109–114
    See also kitchen equipment
training, 21–22
Transfernation, 19
travel memoirs, 51
Try This: Traveling the Globe without Leaving the Table (Freeman), 51
twist, 52

U

Unbroken Ground (Patagonia documentary), 13
United Nations
    on food security, 14
    UNFAO, 111
    World Food Programme, 41
University of Wisconsin-Madison's Safe and Healthy Food Pantries Project, 37
The Unofficial Downton Abbey Cookbook, Revised Edition: From Lady Mary's Crab Canapes to Daisy's Mouse Au Chocolat—More than 150 Recipes from Upstairs and Downstairs (Baines), 78
The Unofficial Harry Potter Cookbook: From Cauldron Cakes to Knickerbocker Glory—More than 150 Magical Recipes for Wizards and Nonwizards Alike (Bucholz), 78
The Unofficial Recipes of the Hunger Games: 187 Recipes Inspired by the Hunger Games, Catching Fire, and Mockingjay (Rockridge University Press), 78

Unsavory Truth: How Food Companies Skew the Science of What We Eat (Nestle), 16
urbn pockets, 41
U.S. Department of Agriculture (USDA)
    on food deserts, 14–15
    research tools from, 35
    Survey Tools website, 36
    tool kits from, 113
    website resources of, 114

V

values, 12–13
vegan diet, 18
"Veganism: Eating Consciously and Compassionately" (McLaurin), 112
vegetables, 80–82
vegetarian diet, 18, 87
Vidgen, Helen, 3–4
Vitamix blender, 80
Vnuk, Rebecca, 97
vocabulary
    See terminology
volunteers
    for community food assessment, 34
    in Edible Education Garden, 81, 82

W

waiter, 26
Walker, D. B., 78
The Walking Dead: The Official Cookbook and Survival Guide (Wilson), 78
Walsh, Alison, 69
Warren Township Branch of Somerset County Library System, 65–67
waste, 18–19
Waste: Uncovering the Global Food Scandal (Stuart), 16
water, 17
Watson, Jené, 55–56
Weber, David, 25
websites
    foodie websites/apps for kids, 41
    interactive websites, took kits, MOOCS, 109–114

WebstaurantStore, 114
The Weeding Handbook: A Shelf-by-Shelf Guide (Vnuk), 97
well-being, 12–13
Wenger, Shaunda, 69
West Boca Branch of Palm Beach County Library System, Boca Raton, Florida, 63–65
Western meals/menu categories, 102
What to Eat? report (Canada), 6
"What's Cooking in Your Food System?: A Guide to Community Food Assessment" (Community Food Security Coalition), 36
"Where Can I Use SNAP EBT?" (USDA), 114
Wilson, Lauren, 78
The Wizard's Cookbook: Magical Recipes Inspired by Harry Potter, Merlin, The Wizard of Oz, and More (Beaupommier), 78
Wolf, Erik, 25
Wookie Cookies: A Star Wars Cookbook (Davis), 78
Woolmer, Annabel, 42
work plan
    Community Food Assessment: Work Plan Template, 106–107
    creation of, 33–34
The World Atlas of Street Food (Quinn), 51
world cuisines, 101
World of Warcraft: The Official Cookbook. (Monroe-Cassel), 78
Wrandman, Richard, 8
Wyshak, Susie, 25

Y

Yes, Chef (Samuelsson), 64
The Young Chef: Recipes and Techniques for Kids Who Love to Cook (Culinary Institute of America), 42
Your Baking Club Checklist, 71
Yummiloo app, 41

Z

"Zero Waste Schools Toolkit" (Seven Generations Ahead), 113

CPSIA information can be obtained
at www.ICGtesting.com
Printed in the USA
LVHW102324050120
642610LV00011B/803/P